Emerging Grassroots Power

About the Author

After obtaining his Honours and Post Graduate Degrees in Philosophy from Calcutta University, M.L. Majumdar taught Philosophy in a degree college in West Bengal before joining the Indian Administrative Service and held many important positions under the State Government of Bihar and the Government of India where his last posting was as Secretary to the Government of India. He had also worked as a short term Consultant for the Commonwealth Secretariat, London. He took retirement from the IAS before joining as State Election Commissioner, Bihar on September 26, 2000.

EMERGING GRASSROOTS POWER

A Critique on Elections to the Panchayats and the Municipalities in Bihar

M. L. MAJUMDAR

Published for

Institute of Social Sciences

by

CONCEPT PUBLISHING COMPANY, NEW DELHI-110059

Cataloging in Publication Data—DK

Courtesy: D.K. Agencies (P) Ltd.<docinfo@dkagencies.com>

Majumdar, M. L.

Emerging grassroots power : a critique on elections to the panchayats and the municipalities in Bihar / M.L. Majumdar.

p. cm.

Includes index.

ISBN 8180691640

1. Elections—India—Bihar. 2. Local government—India—Bihar. I. Title.

324.095 412 21

ISBN-81-8069-164-0

First Published 2005

Published and Printed by
Ashok Kumar Mittal
Concept Publishing Company,
A/15-16, Commercial Block, Mohan Garden,
New Delhi-110059 (INDIA)

Phones : 25351460, 25351794
Fax : 091-11-25357103
Email : publishing@conceptpub.com

Contents

Foreword

2001 was a landmark year for return of grassroots democracy in Bihar with election to the Panchayats and to the Municipalities held after more than two decades. These were significant as these were taking place for the first time after the 73rd and 74th amendments to the Constitution. Last elections to the Panchayats were held in May-June 1978 while that to the municipalities were held in 1985. An impression had been created at the national level that the Government of Bihar was not keen to transfer power, as mandated by the Constitution, to the grassroots institutions, both in the rural and in the urban areas. Another familiar assessment about Bihar Government is that it is a typical case of non-governance.

The author of this book, who was the State Election Commissioner and who conducted two general elections, one to the Panchayats and the other to the municipalities, within one year, has tried to establish that if the final authority takes responsibility for any decision and if such authority gives clear and unambiguous instructions to the district administration, the latter could rise to the occasion and the entire election machinery in the field even though under the administrative control of the State government, would not fail in its duty to carry out the instructions of the Commission in letter and spirit. The author has narrated his personal experiences and his numerous decisions to tackle any contingency to overcome the almost unending challenges faced by him in the conduct of two elections.

The statistical details under various tables as also the appendices have been taken from the report "Grass Root Democracy Incarnate" which is a report on election to the

Panchayats and the municipalities in Bihar prepared by the State Election Commission, Bihar in December 2002.

The author is critical of the various agencies involved in election related work and at the same time he makes an objective analysis of the entire election process and the response of the State government and the district administration including police administration. The author has shown that the voters at grassroots level can no longer be taken for granted and that if the State government and the field administration under it are sincere the stigma that Bihar can never have grassroots democratic institutions in position would be a thing of the past.

The next election to the Panchayats is due early 2006 for which the immediate necessity is to complete the work of delimitation of constituencies. As the work could not have been completed during his tenure, the author chose to quit the post on March 28, 2003, six months ahead of his term's expiry paving the way for the government to appoint his successor who has to initiate the work of delimitation of constituencies immediately.

New Delhi

George Mathew
Director
Institute of Social Sciences

The Author's Dilemma

With the 73rd amendment to the Constitution according legal sanction to the Panchayati Raj Institutions (PRIs) it became imperative on the State government to put the election machinery in place so as to conduct election to the three-tier Panchayat Institutions every five years unless election are otherwise necessitated before the expiry of five years.

Though the Constitution (73rd) Amendment Act, 1992 became effective from April 24, 1993 election to the three-tier PRIs could not be conducted till April-May, 2001. The circumstances responsible for the delay are dealt within the book. Thus when I got a call from a senior bureaucrat of the State government to agree to take over as State Election Commissioner it was a very difficult choice for me to react immediately. I got the request in February, 2000 while the tenure of the present State Election Commissioner was to expire on April 14, 2000. I was posted in the Central government as Secretary to the Government of India and I had already decided to settle down in Calcutta after retirement. I sought time to give my reaction which was granted. After due deliberation and consultations with my wife and two sons I decided not to accept the offer. The reasons for my refusal were as follows.

In most of the major States the tenure of appointment of the State Election Commissioner is five years with an upper age limit of 65 years. Bihar was perhaps the only major State where the maximum tenure of appointment of the State Election Commissioner is only three years with an upper age limit of 62 years. Since the age limit of IAS officers was raised to 60 years as against 58 years earlier, I did not consider the offer reasonable as it is very difficult, nay, impossible, for an officer to devise, in such a short time, an elaborate and reasonably fool-proof system for conducting election to the PRIs. My reasoning was that assuming I would be able to conduct one PRIs election I must also get an opportunity to utilize the experience so gained to improve subsequent election procedures. I was fully aware that immediately after the election to the PRIs, election to the Urban Local Bodies (ULBs) would be scheduled which would be difficult for me to ignore and at the same time I would not get time to complete the likely election to the ULBs. Through newspaper reports it was clear that the Patna High Court, while hearing a Public Interest Litigation (PIL), was monitoring on regular basis the steps taken by the State government in completing election to the PRIs. I knew that as the State Election Commissioner I would be under the constitutional obligation to conduct elections to PRIs and ULBs. I visualized that I would not be able to do justice to the post and hence declined the offer.

The other reason for refusal was that I was not very sure about the capabilities of the District Magistrates (DMs), Block Development Officers (BDOs) and other officers and staff posted under the District Administration to conduct the actual election. Newspaper reports from time to time had created an impression that the civil servants, specially those belonging to the two premier All India Services, i.e. Indian Administrative Service (IAS) and the Indian Police Service (IPS), particularly those posted in the district, were politically aligned with one group or the other and, therefore, to expect a fair deal from such officers was very much suspected. Though I was a member of the IAS of Bihar cadre, I had been mostly posted under the Government of India in New Delhi since September, 1980 except for a brief three years period when I held two important positions under the State government at Patna. Thus I had very little personal knowledge about the officers who joined the service after mid eighties and these are also the officers who would be mostly posted as District Magistrates and Superintendents of Police (SPs) in the district who would be directly involved in the conduct of any election, whether to the PRIs or to the State Legislature or the Parliament. Thus the image of the IAS and IPS officers, self-created and reinforced by various newspaper reports, did not infuse any confidence in me to do justice to the post of State Election Commissioner.

The last reason for saying no, was purely personal and family related with my wife Ranjita putting forward her convincing argument against my taking up the assignment at Patna. After all a break in journey is not justified if the trouble is not worth it.

I, therefore, conveyed my decision to the senior bureaucrat of the State government who was also one of my closest friends. His first reaction was of disbelief as it was beyond anybody's comprehension how one could decline such a lucrative post-retirement job. He tried to argue that it would be worthwhile to work even for two years rather than remain without work immediately after retirement. Since we already have got two years extra bonus, thanks to the Fifth Pay Commission recommendations, I was not convinced by my friend's argument. Still persuading that a retired IAS officer has no value, he gave his own logic that after retirement the officer becomes an electric bulb which, once fused, becomes absolutely useless. I jokingly told him that in India everything is recycled and is put to better use and more often than not re-cycled materials become more useful, if not stronger, than the original.

My friend in Patna did not give up. He then suggested that the present three-year tenure of the State Election Commissioner could be enhanced to four years or even to five years and the upper age limit could also be increased accordingly. Bewildered by his persistence I straightaway asked him as to why he was so insistent on me. His candid reply was "you are very steadfast in your approach and whatever work you take on hand you complete." I knew he was the last person to flatter me and what he said could be genuine. I also believed that he would follow-up on his assurance of extending the tenure and the upper age limit of the State Election Commissioner but I do not think he ever made any serious efforts as only upper age limit was made 64 years. But I have no regrets as I have completed my job reasonably well.

After his last request I sought some time. One morning in July, 2000, my friend suddenly called me and sought my final response immediately. Since my wife was at her morning prayers I was unable to talk to her and gestured about the call. She came out and opined that since the State government felt that I would be competent to do the job I should take it as an appreciation and accept the offer. I conveyed my willingness to my friend who was still on phone but told him that I would do so only after taking retirement from the IAS.

Finally, I took over as the third State Election Commissioner of Bihar on September 26, 2000 and thence began my odyssey which ended with elections to the Urban Local Bodies in June, 2002. I, thus, conducted two general elections, one to the rural and other to the urban Local Bodies, within a period of about one year, after two decades.

1

Introduction

Village Panchayat, the lowest unit of the Local Self-Government in the rural areas, was already in existence and the State of Bihar was known for an effectively functioning three-tier Panchayati Raj Institutions (PRIs) in the rural areas. Prior to the 73rd amendment to the Constitution of India effective from 24th April, 1993, the PRIs did not have any constitutional status.

The structure of the three-tier PRIs would be explained subsequently as we proceed further. It will be enough at this stage to state that the Gram Panchayat which is the lowest unit of the PRIs in the rural areas is the most effective unit of the Local Self-Government. The Mukhiya (chairperson) of the Gram Panchayat was and is still the kingpin at the grassroots level. I still very clearly remember the occasion when I was so embarrassed to notice that the Mukhiya of the local Gram Panchayat was already there with the immediately required relief materials for the flood affected people way back in the night of probably the month of October, 1968 when as a young civil servant, a member of the Indian Administrative Service, I was posted as the Sub-Divisional Magistrate of Supaul (now a district) under the district of Saharsa, in north Bihar which is subject to devastating flood of the river Kosi every year. The sudden discharge of 1.3 million cusecs of water, supposed to be the highest till then, flooded the entire area within the two embankments of the river Kosi and the people were living on the roofs of the houses. People who managed to come to the eastern embankment for shelter were getting instant relief provided by the Mukhiya of the local Gram Panchayat whom I met after midnight even though as the Sub Divisional Magistrate I was supposed to be there immediately with my officers and relief materials. What I am trying to make out here is that the institution of Gram Panchayat with the Mukhiya as its head was very much in existence and Mukhiya was one of the most popular figures in the rural area. That most of these Mukhiyas represented the feudal elements of the society was an altogether different matter.

Prior to the 73rd amendment to the Constitution, the holding of election to the PRIs was subject to the executive decision of the Government and the last election to the PRIs prior to the 73rd amendment to the Constitution was held during May/June, 1978. There was no election during the intervening period ending March, 2001 even though the amended provisions of the Constitution make it mandatory for the State government to conduct election to the PRIs every five years. An attempt was made to hold election to the PRIs in 1996 but the judgement and order of the Patna High Court dated 19th March, 1996 provided a good excuse to the political executive to postpone elections.

1978 elections witnessed large scale violence and reportedly more than 700 people were killed during the election. Thus when under fear of stricture from the High Court the State government decided to conduct election to the PRIs, apprehension of large scale violence during election was predicted and highlighted by the print media. Very important and well-informed people made public statements predicting a casualty figure of more than 5,000 during election. There was all round cynicism that there would be no election in Bihar and even if election could take place there would be lot of bloodshed. That free and fair election to the PRIs was held in April, 2001, after 23 years, is altogether a different matter.

With such widely reported apprehension of large scale violence, it was a stupendous task for the State Election Commission (Commission), which is still a nascent body without any previous experience of conducting elections to the PRIs, to discharge the constitutional responsibilities to conduct election to the PRIs. The Commission faced almost non-ending hurdles in the conduct of elections.

There is mandatory provision in the Constitution for reservation for the post of member and offices of chairpersons of the Panchayats in all the three tiers for the Scheduled Castes, the Scheduled Tribes and women. The vested interests filed writ petitions in the Patna High Court and the High Court *vide* its order dated 19th March, 1996 declared that there cannot be any reservation for the post of chairpersons as such a post is single in nature and, therefore, reservation will amount to 100 per cent reservation which is not permissible under the law. The State government filed a Special Leave Petition (SLP) before the Supreme Court and the same is pending for the last 7 years for a decision. Every State of the country has implemented the constitutional mandate of reservation for the post of member and offices of chairperson in favour of the above categories of persons. Thus, Bihar has the singular distinction of being the only State in the country where a validly subsisting constitutional mandate is not implemented. The fact is that the prevailing socio-economic backwardness of the weaker sections of the population and the women in general specially in the rural areas fully justifies reservation in favour of such categories of persons for the offices of chairpersons of the PRIs. Since chairperson is the most effective office bearer, SC, ST and women chairperson will make all the difference in the rural areas. The Commission moved the Supreme Court for the required permission to comply with the constitutional mandate for reservation for the offices of chairperson. The State government did not support the Commission and it opted to remain neutral. The Supreme Court declined to grant the permission to the Commission. However, reservation as per the constitutional provision could be enforced for the post of member of the PRIs.

The political leadership of the State was reluctant to usher in grassroots democracy, their public posture to the contrary notwithstanding. When the election schedule was announced, a large number of writ petitions were filed in the Patna High

Court challenging various decisions of the Commission which remained bogged down in filing show cause to the writ petitions. At times, it created an impression that election might have to be deferred. However, ultimately the Commission succeeded in getting favourable decisions from the High Court.

With such endless obstacles in the way, it was a miracle that the Commission could conduct not only a free and fair election but also an election which can be reasonably characterised as violence-free. Thus, election to the three-tier PRIs held in April, 2001 after a gap of 23 years was a landmark one in every respect. The State of Bihar has a high crime graph with more than 10 casualties per day on an average, it was a great relief that the casualty figures during the entire process of election did not cross even 100.

As in the case of PRIs, the State had in the past functioning municipalities but election to the Urban Local Bodies (ULBs) was not regular as it was entirely dependent on the executve decision of the State government. The last election to the municipalities was held in early 80s and thereafter there was no election till April, 2002. The 74th amendment to the Constitution effective from January 6, 1993 accorded constitutional status to the municipalities and it became mandatory for the State government to conduct periodical elections. After the successful conduct of election to PRIs, the State government could not find any escape route to avoid election to the ULBs. There was pressure from the articulate section of the population in urban areas for the conduct of election to the ULBs after the elected PRIs came into existence. Apprehension was expressed and highlighted by the print media that there would be large scale violence during election to the municipalities for the reason that the urban people would remain alert and they would create large scale disturbance. All these apprehensions proved totally wrong and elections to all the five municipal corporations, 32 municipalities and 80 Nagar Panchayats were held in April, 2002. Elections to the ULBs were almost violence-free as only three casualties took place in Gaya Municipal Corporation area. It has been acclaimed by all that the election was free and fair.

With the elections to the PRIs and ULBs, the democratic institutions of local self-governance at the grassroots level, both in the urban and the rural areas, came into existence. The constitutional mandate of holding elections of the PRIs and the ULBs could be complied with.

2

Structure of the PRIs

The Bihar Panchayat Raj Act, 1993 (Act) provides the legal basis for the constitution and composition of the three-tier Panchayat Institutions. At the bottom of the three-tier structure is the Gram Panchayat (village Panchayat) with a population roughly between 6,500 and 7,500, at the intermediate level is a Panchayat Samiti (Block level Panchayat) which is co-terminus with the geographical area of the concerned community development Block and at the top of the three-tier is the Zila Parishad (District Panchayat) which is co-terminus with the geographical area of the district. Thus while the population of a Gram Panchayat is decided by the State government as per the provisions of the Act taking into account various considerations including the geographical boundaries, social conditions of the population etc., the population of a Panchayat Samiti and that of a Zila Parishad are the population of the Block/District concerned as per the census figures. The existing PRIs are based on the 1991 census population in terms of the legal provisions.

A Gram Panchayat comprises one or more than one village depending on the population and the prevailing geographical conditions. Every village, comprised within the area of a panchayat, has a provision of a "Gram Sabha", i.e., a Village Assembly, which is a body consisting of persons registered in the electoral rolls of the village. Thus a Gram Panchayat may have as many Gram Sabhas as there are villages within its area. A Gram Sabha may exercise such powers and perform such functions at the village level as provided for in the law enacted by the Legislature of the State. These persons registered in the electoral rolls are also the voters who directly elect the chairperson and other members of the Gram Panchayat as also the members of the other panchayats in the three-tier system. Therefore, any aspirant for the above posts of the Panchayats has to give due importance to the opinion of the Gram Sabha.

A Gram Panchayat consists of the Mukhiya who is elected directly by the voters and the directly elected members representing various territorial constituencies (wards) comprising approximately 500 population per ward besides certain ex-officio members such as the local MLAs, MLCs and MPs. It would be necessary to elaborate the significance of the word 'Mukhiya', i.e., the Chairperson of Gram Panchayat. The Mukhiya is directly elected as stated above. There is a reason behind calling the Chairperson of a Gram Panchayat as Mukhiya. In the rural areas of Bihar usually the head of the family or the head of the village is addressed as Mukhiyaji in common parlance. Thus the villagers are very familiar with the word 'Mukhiya' which, no doubt, denotes the elected Chairperson of the Gram Panchayat, but it also has its own connotation in local parlance. The Act has, therefore, taken cognizance of this commonly understood word Mukhiya to denote the directly elected Chairperson of the Gram Panchayat. In fact, Mukhiya has become the kingpin of the entire Panchayat system and it is he who can change the lot of the rural areas through his own personal efforts and thereby become the real friend, philosopher and guide for the entire population of the Gram Panchayat he represents.

The Panchayat Samiti (Block level Samiti), i.e., Panchayat at the intermediate level, consists of the directly elected members from the territorial constituencies (wards) with a population of approximately 5,000 for each ward with the *ex officio* members who include local MLAs, MLCs and the MPs and the Mukhiyas of the Gram Panchayats within the Panchayat Samiti area. The Chief of the Panchayat Samiti is called Pramukh and he is one of the directly elected members of the Samiti. Same is the case with the Up-Pramukh or the

Deputy Chief of the Panchayat Samiti. Under the provisions of the Constitution it is not mandatory for smaller States having a population not exceeding two million to constitute intermediate level Panchayats.

The Zila Parishad (District Panchayat), i.e., Panchayat at the highest level in the three-tier structure, consists of directly elected members representing various territorial constituencies (wards) with approximately 50,000 population per ward besides ex-officio members like the local MLAs, MLCs, MPs of the District as also the Pramukhs or chief of all the Panchayat Samitis in the district. The Chairperson of the Zila Parishad is called Adhyaksha who is one of the directly elected members of the Zila Parishad which also elects one amongst them as the Upadhyaksha or the Vice-Chairman of the Zila Parishad.

For the purpose of election, a Gram Panchayat is sub-divided into more than one territorial constituencies (wards) in accordance with the provisions of the Act and the Rules. A Panchayat Samiti, i.e., a Panchayat at the intermediate level shall comprise of more than one ward of the Gram Panchayats within its area. Likewise, the Zila Parishad (Panchayat at the highest level) shall comprise more than one ward of the Panchayat Samitis within its area. While combining more than one ward of a Gram Panchayat it must be ensured that no ward of a Gram Panchayat is sub-divided. This means that every ward of a Panchayat Samiti or Zila Parishad shall comprise certain number of wards of Gram Panchayats so as to fulfil the requirement of the population figure of the Panchayat Samiti or the Zila Parishad, as the case may be. The rationale behind keeping the ward of a Gram Panchayat intact is that every elected member of a Panchayat Samiti and of the Zila Parishad shall represent the entire population of the particular ward of the concerned Gram Panchayat. In other words, the entire population of the ward of a Gram Panchayat know who their elected member of the Panchayat Samiti (or the Zila Parishad) is.

One would notice that the three tiers of the Panchayats have different nomenclatures for chairperson/vice chairperson and each has been so selected to remove confusion. For example, the word Mukhiya literary means head man, but for the people of the rural areas, however, the word Mukhiya carries a specific connotation and, therefore, the same has been adopted by the Legislature to avoid confusion.

To maintain the supremacy of the elected members at the grassroots level the Act does not give the ex-officio members of the Panchayat at each level any voting rights in the election or removal of Chairperson or Vice-Chairperson of the Panchayat concerned. It is the sole prerogative of the elected members of a Panchayat to elect one amongst themselves as the Chairperson (except the Chairperson of a Gram Panchayat who is elected directly) and the Vice-Chairperson or to remove such office bearers through a motion of no-confidence. This effectively means that the influential ex-officio members (MPs and MLAs) cannot impose their proxy candidate on the Panchayat as Chairperson/Vice-Chairperson. These ex-officio members, nevertheless, made an attempt to attend the first meeting of the elected members to elect office-bearers on the plea that they would only be present in the meeting without participating therein. Some of these ex-officio members took up the matter with me. Since their game plan was too obvious, I asked the District Magistrates to ensure that the ex-officio members not be allowed anywhere near the meeting place. Thus one more attempt by the vested interests to browbeat the grassroots democrats was thwarted.

3

State Election Commission

Administrative and Physical Infrastructure

As stated earlier, the 73rd amendment to the Constitution added one chapter on the Panchayats and accordingly Articles 243 to 243-O were added to the Constitution. These amended (newly added) Articles in the Constitution provide for the constitution of Panchayats at the village level and at other levels and administrative machinery with the State Election Commission at the head for the conduct of elections to the Panchayats. The Articles also provide for reservation of seats and offices of Chairpersons of the Panchayats at each level in favour of the Scheduled Castes, the Scheduled Tribes and women as also the manner of calculating such reserved posts. The Constitution also empowers the Legislature of the State to make law to carry out the provisions of the Constitution. In terms of the provisions of the Constitution the State Legislature passed the Bihar Panchayati Raj Act, 1993 referred to earlier. The State government also framed Bihar Panchayat Election Rules, 1995 (Rules).

Thus the Constitution, the Act and the Rules lay down the administrative infrastructure for the conduct of election to the Panchayats. Clause (1) of Article 243-K of the Constitution vests superintendence, direction and control of the preparation of electoral rolls for, and the conduct of, all elections to the Panchayats in a State Election Commission consisting of a State Election Commissioner. The State Election Commissioner is to be appointed by the Governor of the State. Similar provisions have been made in section 136 of the Act.

Article 243-K of the Constitution and section 136 of the Act are reproduced below:

243-K. Elections of the Panchayats

1. The superintendence direction and control of the preparation of electoral rolls for, and the conduct of, all elections to the Panchayats shall be vested in a State Election Commission consisting of a State Election Commissioner to be appointed by the Governor.
2. Subject to the provisions of any law made by the Legislature of a State, the conditions of service and tenure of office of the State Election Commissioner shall be such as the Governor may by rule determine: Provided that the State Election Commissioner shall not be removed from his office except in like manner and on the like grounds as a judge of a High Court and the conditions of service of the State Election Commissioner shall not be varied to his disadvantage after his appointment.
3. The Governor of a State shall, when so requested by the State Election Commission, make available to the State Election Commission such staff as may be necessary for the discharge of the functions conferred on the State Election Commission by clause (1).
4. Subject to the provisions of this Constitution, the Legislature of a State may, by law, make provision with respect to all matters relating to, or in connection with, elections to the Panchayats.

Section 136. State Election Commission

1. There shall be a State Election Commission appointed by the Governor for superintendence, direction and control of the preparation of electoral rolls for, and the conduct of all elections to the Panchayat bodies in the State under this act and the rules made

thereunder. The Commission shall consist of a State Election Commissioner to be appointed by the governor.

2. The conditions of services and tenures of office of the State Election Commissioner shall be such as the Governor may by rule determine:
   Provided that the State Election Commissioner shall not be removed from his office except in like manner and on the like grounds as a Judge of the High Court and the conditions of service of the State Election Commissioner shall not be varied to his disadvantage after his appointment.
3. The Government shall, when so requested by the State Election Commission, make available to the State Election Commission such staff as may be necessary for the discharge of the functions conferred on the State Election Commission under this Act.

If we look at the provisions of clause (1) of Article 324 of the Constitution vesting similar power in the Election Commission of India, a distinct similarity will be noticed. The State Election Commission is responsible for the conduct of elections to the Panchayat Institutions and to the municipalities as per the provisions of Article 243-K and Article 243-ZA respectively. The Election Commission of India is, on the other hand, responsible for election to the Parliament and State Legislatures as also to the offices of the President and the Vice President of India.

The intention of the law makers is very clear. Like the Election Commission of India, the State Election Commission shall be an independent constitutional body outside the government so that it can conduct elections to the Panchayats and the municipalities without any fear or favour. The wordings of proviso to clause (2) of Article 243-K make the concept of independence of the Commission explicit as the State Election Commissioner cannot be removed from his office except in like manner and on the like grounds as a Judge of a High Court which, in effect, means the same elaborate procedure of impeachment in both Houses of the Parliament prescribed for similar action in respect of a Judge of the Supreme Court under clause (4) of Article 124 of the Constitution. As a further safeguard, it has also been provided that the conditions of the services of the Commissioner shall not be varied to his disadvantage after his appointment. Section 136 of the Act passed by the Bihar State Legislature makes similar provisions in respect of the State Election Commissioner.

While the Parliament in its wisdom voted for complete independence of the Commission, the same has not been appreciated by the political leadership in the State even though the State government has got an Act passed by the State Legislature. The State Election Commission virtually means the State Election Commissioner as it is a one-member Commission to be appointed by the Governor of the State and all the powers of the Commission under the Constitution and the Act are vested in the Commissioner. Though the Constitution envisages complete independence of the Commission, it is silent about the tenure of appointment and the eligibility for the appointment of the Commissioner. Apparently the State government has taken advantage of such loopholes and accordingly the State has taken over the powers to decide tenure of the Commissioner through the rules relating to the appointment and service conditions of the State Election Commissioner. The rules provide that the tenure of the State Election Commissioner shall be three years provided that the Commissioner shall demit his office on attaining the age of 62 years which has now been revised to sixty four years on my insistence before agreeing to the offer of appointment. A well informed source in the government confessed privately that left to themselves the political leadership would prefer a tenure of one year only for the State Election Commissioner with the provision of yearly extension to ensure a genuinely pliable officer in the post. Bihar is perhaps the only major State which has the least tenure of three years of the Commissioner with the upper age limit being 62 years originally, now revised upto 64 years while most of the States provide for a tenure of five years with an upper age limit of 65 years. The advantage of longer tenure ensures subsequent use of experience.

Under the provisions of the Constitution the next general election to the Panchayats will be due in April-May, 2006 unless unavoidable reasons necessitate election earlier. As stated earlier, the composition of Gram Panchayat at the moment is based on the 1991 census population. However, as per provisions of the Constitution and the Act the next election would be on the basis of 2001 census. Thus the number of Panchayats will substantially increase from the present figure of 8,471 on the basis of increase of 28.33 per cent of the population in the rural areas. The same is the case for the Municipalities, the next election for which is due in May-June, 2007. This increase in population would mean that the Government has to take a decision about reorganization of the Panchayats and in all probability the number of Panchayats would increase substantially as with a large population a Gram Panchayat would be ill-suited to do any meaningful developmental activity in the Panchayat. Whether the government decides to reorganize the Panchayat or not, the delimitation of constituencies (wards) is essential and on a rough estimate the existing number of 1,16,029 wards of the Gram Panchayats would have to be reorganized into about 1,50,000 wards in addition to the wards of the Panchayat Samitis and Zila Parishads. Since during last election it was noticed that the rural people were playing an active role in the Panchayat election one can imagine the risk involved in changing the boundaries of the constituencies as any change in the configuration of population of various wards would affect the prospect of many candidates. The Commission got several complaints about the ward formation and preparation of voters list during election to the Panchayat in April-May, 2001. At that time the Commission took the plea that as per the provisions of the Act the Commission was not in a position to make any change in the delimitation of the constituencies and the finally published voters list after the notification for election to the Panchayats was issued by the Governor. This plea cannot be taken at the time of next election in early 2006.

Besides the reorganization of the Panchayats to be done by the State government and delimitation of constituencies to be done by the Commission, there are certain other steps like selection of polling stations, identification of constituencies to be reserved for the Scheduled Castes, the Scheduled Tribes and women in addition to the preparation of electoral rolls to be completed latest by December, 2005, so as to allow the Commission to conduct the election during April-May, 2006. Parliamentary election will be due in 2004 and election to the State Legislative Assembly in March, 2005 and, therefore, the district administration would be fully pre-occupied with Parliamentary and Assembly election for about six to eight months during 2004-2005 with limited time of little over two years for the State government and the Commission to complete the preliminary work for the next elections to the Panchayats.

To complete the above work in time, the Commission would be required to prepare detailed guidelines for delimitation of constituencies and to impart practical training to the District Election officers and the Block Development officers. Thus detailed guidelines should be issued and the training should be completed in a time bound manner so that the actual work of delimitation can start from November, 2003. The rural people will take a keen interest and will remain alert during the delimitation of constituencies and the field administration will be under tremendous pressure to ensure that the job is done reasonably well. The State government has been kept informed of the magnitude of the work. This will be a new and challenging work for the next Commissioner who will otherwise be benefited by the detailed and elaborate guidelines issued by me during the elections to the Panchayats and the municipalities. All these guidelines, circulars etc. have been printed in the form of compendia and are available with the field officers besides a report titled "Grass Root Democracy Incarnate" which narrates the circumstances under which two elections were conducted and also the reasons for taking certain decisions. As stated earlier, the Commission is a one-man body and without any intention of taking the credit, I would like to state here that every circular etc. issued by the Commission as also the report published by the Commission had been dictated by me personally and it had been a very strenuous job considering the fact that I had no previous experience of conducting election to the Panchayats which had not taken place in Bihar since May-June, 1978.

The terms and conditions of service of the State Election Commissioner are reasonably liberal. The Commission has also been delegated full financial powers by the government except that for the purchase of a new vehicle, prior approval of the government would be necessary. The Commissioner is also entitled to a rent free fully furnished accommodation befitting his status besides additional pension for the duration of the service as State Election Commissioner provided he has completed at least two years in the post. This pension is in addition to the pension that the Commissioner would be otherwise drawing, if any, for the post he held earlier. An otherwise independent Commission, the government, nevertheless, created some avoidable obstacles, which were more for ego satisfaction than any mental satisfaction. When I refer to government I mean the highest decision making authority in the government on a particular matter and not the administrative department of the Commission, i.e., the Department of Panchayati Raj, the incumbent officers of which have been a great source of strength to the Commission and to me personally. The Panchayati Raj Department has extended all possible assistance to the Commission and in fact during election to the Panchayats in April-May, 2001 the department became almost an extension of the Commission and there could not have been better coordination between the Commission and the department.

The Commission has small manpower base. Besides the State Election Commissioner. The government has sanctioned the following posts:

Sl. No.	*Designation of the Posts*	*Number of Sanctioned Posts*	*Pay-scale (Revised)*
1.	Joint Election Commissioner	1	14300-18300
2.	Secretary	1	12000-16500
3.	Deputy Secretary	1	12000-16500
4.	Secretary to Commissioner	1	10000-15200
5.	Accounts Officer	1	6500-10500
6.	Public Relation Officer	1	6500-10500
7.	Private Secretary	1	6500-10500
8.	Registrar	1	6500-10500
9.	Asstt. Statistical Officer	1	5500-9000
10.	Section Officer	2	6500-10500
11.	Junior Statistical Assistant	1	5000-8000
12.	Personal Assistant	5	5500-9000
13.	Secretariat Assistant	10	5500-9000
14.	Computer Operator	2	5000-8000
15.	Accountant	2	5000-8000
16.	Typist	3	4000-6000
17.	Bill Clerk	1	4000-6000
18.	Routine Clerk	2	4000-6000
19.	Vehicle Driver	3	3050-4590
20.	Treasury Messenger	1	2750-4400
21.	Orderly/Peon	10	2550-3200

The Commission did not experience any difficulty in conducting two elections, one to the Panchayats and the other to the municipalities, with such a small contingent of manpower. The Commission could also draw the required number of personnel from any government organization whenever necessary. Many State Election Commissions have an IAS officer in super time scale as Secretary to the Commission who is also the Chief Executive Officer and the Administrative head of the office. Considering the financial power delegated to the Commission, the seniority of the three officers below the Commissioner is considered inadequate. Moreover, all the three officers are in the same rank belonging to the State Civil Service and, therefore, there could be inter-personal equation problem among the officers. Further, the rationale of having a post of Joint Election Commissioner is not clear. The post has no relevance in the scheme of things.

Though the Commission has been delegated full financial power of the government it has no administrative power to make appointment even to such lower level post as peons, drivers etc. The Secretary of a Department or the Head of a Directorate under the State government is authorized to make appointments to such lower level posts as above. In all fairness, the Commission, which is a constitutional body, should have been delegated at least such administrative power which are exercised by the Secretary of a department, which will also be in tune with the financial power delegated to the Commission. The reasons for not delegating this power are not clear.

While administrative infrastructure did not create any insurmountable difficulties in conducting the election it is the physical infrastructure, i.e., the office accommodation and the residential accommodation for the Commissioner, which created serious problems as the office staff and the officers, including the Commissioner became vulnerable to unruly visitors as the polling days came nearer.

The total space for office purpose was adequate but its location was not safe from security point of view for a constitutional body like this. The office was located in a commercial building on third floor and there was no independent entry to the office complex with the result that the security personnel on duty were not effective in controlling the visitors. Moreover, being situated in a small place the security personnel armed with fire arms were themselves vulnerable as any use of fire arms in such a congested place would have created serious law and order problem. Even security personnel with lathis could not be effective because of the same reasons.

When the people realized that elections to the Panchayats were finally taking place the number of visitors, including women, increased manifold and it became difficult for the office staff to control them. The entire office staff had to undergo a harrowing experience.

Originally the State government allotted an old residential building as office accommodation at 7, Kranti Marg which as such is a convenient place. Besides being grossly inadequate the building itself is in a very bad shape and requires major repairs. The Commissioner himself verbally brought to the notice of the persons who matter in the government about the need for repairing the old building and construction of two small barracks for which the total cost was estimated by the State Building Construction Department at about Rs. three million and the department would have taken only few months to complete the job. Government remained totally indifferent to such a small request of the Commission even though there was full justification for a separate and independent office accommodation for the Commission which has come to be a permanent body. The indifference of the government later became so clear that even when the Planning Commission of India (later verbally conveyed to the Commissioner) agreed to sanction A.C.A. (Additional Central Plan Assistance) amounting to around Rs. 10 million estimated to be the cost of a new office building if such a proposal would be sent by the State government in consultation with the Commission, the State government, to the knowledge of the Commission, preferred not to make any specific proposal.

Besides the office accommodation, the residential accommodation of the Commissioner was equally vulnerable during the peak period of the election. As per the terms and conditions of appointment of the Commissioner he is entitled to a fully furnished rent free accommodation befitting his status. The previous State Election Commissioner occupied a government bungalow which was vacated before I joined the post but it never occurred to the government that this vacant house could have been kept ready for occupation by the next Commissioner even though the government was fully aware that the next Commissioner would be joining very soon. An assurance was given that after the creation of Jharkhand on November 15, 2000 when many government bungalows would fall vacant, the Commissioner would be given a suitable accommodation. However, this assurance was fulfilled only in June 2001 after the entire election process was over.

I am referring to the inadequacy of the physical

infrastructure only to emphasize that the entire Commission remained under stress not so much because of work involved as on account of the perceived sense of insecurity. But I am happy that my officers and staff faced the situation bravely and it goes to the credit of the visitors that they also appreciated the sincerity and impartiality of the Commission in its work and they did not create any unseemly scenes. As the voting process started in the beginning of April 2001 things changed for the better.

4

The Challenges

The State government, by a notification dated March 30, 1994 constituted the State Election Commission. Sri K.K. Saha, a retired IAS officer held this post for three years upto January 22, 1997 whereafter Sri J.L. Arya, another retired IAS officer was appointed as the State Election Commissioner and he held the post from April 15, 1997 to April 14, 2000. As the third Commissioner I assumed charge of the post on September 26, 2000. Thus there was no Commissioner for nearly five months. Mr. Saha completed the preliminary work, including printing of ballot papers, for the conduct of Panchayat elections in early 1996. However, due to the judgement and the order passed by the Patna High Court on March 19,1996 the election had to be deferred. The State government filed a Special Leave Petition (SLP) in the Supreme Court against the above order of the High Court which is pending final decision. Thus except delimitation of constituencies, revision of voters list and selection of polling stations, the Commission did not frame any detailed guidelines for the conduct of election. Somehow or the other, an impression has been created by the political leadership, specially those opposed to the ruling party, that the State government was not serious about the election and they also thought that the Commission was also not serious about its job. It was under these circumstances I was expected to complete the election which people viewed with a lot of suspicion.

Immediately after my assuming the charge of State Election Commissioner, a very prominent political leader, a product of the 1974 JP agitation, reminded me telephonically that as a State government employee I should not toe the line of the State government which did not want election to the Panchayats. When I told him that I was not a State government employee his immediate reply was that since I was an IAS officer it hardly made any difference. When I told him that I was no longer a member of IAS he outrightly dismissed my claim to be out of the control of the Government. I lost my cool, and told him that as an important legislator he should first study the provisions of the Constitution specially Article 243-K and the provisions of the Bihar Panchayati Raj Act passed by the State Legislature of which he was a part. The matter ended there and as the election process progressed the same person changed his opinion completely and unhesitatingly appreciated the independent and impartial role of the Commission.

Therefore, the biggest challenge I faced in my long career as a civil servant was to establish the credibility of the State Election Commission which was, no doubt, more than six years old but still a nascent body without any experience of conducting election to the Panchayats in a State where elections to the Panchayats were last held in 1978. Since the Commission is a one-member body which means only the Commissioner, my personal reputation was at stake as any failure on the part of the Commission would mean my personal failure and no civil servant would like such an eventuality at the end of his career. There was no precedent in the Commission about the circulars, guidelines etc. except those relating to delimitation of constituencies, revision of electoral rolls and selection of polling stations. The real problem in the entire exercise starts with the process of filing of nominations and ends with counting of votes and declaration of results for which the Commission did not have any circulars or instructions. The very idea that I would be required to draft guidelines was quite frightening. Thus to prove the capabilities of the Commission to conduct election, in short, establishing the independent identity of the Commission and its competence to conduct election in a free, fair and impartial manner was the biggest challenge before the Commission.

In the absence of any election to the local bodies in the State for more than two decades, even many of the State government departments, not to speak of the common people, were not aware that there indeed existed a State Election Commission. In fact, as late as February 2001, when the election process had already started, many senior officers of the State government had the impression that the State Election Commissioner was like any other commissioner rank IAS officer heading a government department, i.e., an officer in the pay scale of that of a Joint Secretary to the Government of India.

As indicated earlier, the Commission is a small organization with small manpower. Therefore, the administrative machinery of the State government is also the administrative machinery for the Commission to conduct the election. Under the provisions of the Constitution and the Act the Commission can requisition the services of the State government officers and staff for the conduct of election and over a period of more than 50 years the District Administration has gathered enough experience to conduct election to the State Legislature and to the Parliament. The problems of election to the Panchayats at the grassroots level are completely different which will be clear as we proceed.

Much water has flowed down the Ganges since the last Panchayat elections held in 1978. Therefore, the complexity that I could visualize was enormous.

The District Magistrates who are also the District Election officers under the Act are in overall control of the election machinery within the District. Usually the Block Development officers are the Returning Officers and for members of the Zila Parishad the Sub-Divisional Magistrates are generally notified as Returning Officers. Thus more than 99 per cent Returning Officers are the Block Development Officers who are the officers belonging to the State Civil Service at the junior level except in certain Blocks where officers from the State Agriculture Service are also posted as Block Development Officers. Therefore, none of the BDOs who acted as the Returning Officers for the post of Mukhiya, member of Gram Panchayat and member of Panchayat Samiti, numbering about 1,35,000 posts, was in government service and they might well have been students in the upper classes of school or in the colleges during 1978 when the last election to the Panchayats was held. Likewise, none of the District Magistrates, except a limited number of them, who might have the experience of conducting election to the Panchayats in 1978, if by chance they were posted as BDOs at that time, had any experience of conducting election to the Panchayats. One could very well imagine the challenge that an inexperienced Commission with equally inexperienced District Administration would face in conducting election.

Yet not so irrelevant was the general cynicism of the political leadership who were totally opposed to giving the constitutional power to the grassroots people, their public posture to the contrary notwithstanding. People in general did not take serious note of government announcement of a poll schedule. The print media also projected a negative image of the State government about its intention to conduct election. In this atmosphere it was but natural for me to doubt any prospect of conducting election, much less a free and fair one.

The only ray of hope in an otherwise gloomy atmosphere was that the Patna High Court was regularly monitoring the steps being taken by the State government for the conduct of election to the Panchayats and the court made its intention very clear about the need for early conduct of election to the Panchayats after the interim order of the Supreme Court on August 29, 2000 after hearing certain Interlocutory Applications filed by the Union of India and by the State of Bihar to which I would refer later. The State of Bihar had been denied about Rs. 4000 million every year in the form of Central grants as per the formula of devolution of fund from the Union government to States. These funds are to be utilized by the PRIs and ULBs. In the absence of election to these local bodies, the State was unable to claim such funds. Hence, it was imperative that elections to the Panchayats and the municipalities should take place at the earliest so that various developmental activities could take place in rural and urban areas for which specific financial packages are available. I became quite optimistic about the possibility of conducting election to the Panchayats. But a disinformation campaign was also going on, thanks to the vested interests opposed to devolution of powers to the Panchayats, that ultimately election would not be held. The general assessment was that some people would obtain stay order from the courts. Some of the District Magistrates later confessed to me privately that they were made to believe by some important persons in authority that they should not take the election work seriously as it would be stayed any time after mid-January, 2001. My filing an Interlocutory Application (IA) in the Supreme Court in December, 2000, dealt with in chapter 7, made these vested interests entertain their fond hope that the Apex Court would surely stay the election process as the issues raised in the IA were so relevant that the Court would have no option but to decide the IA. Since any decision on the IA would amount to pre-judging the SLP filed by the State government in the Supreme Court on similar issues, referred to earlier, the vested interests found it most convincing that the Apex Court would take up the SLP filed by the State government along with the IA and this would take time and hence their irresistible conclusion was that the election process would be stayed till the final disposal of the SLP. One District Magistrate later told me in confidence that some senior cabinet ministers had advised him not to take the election work seriously as the stay order was expected anytime, even a possible date around January 15, 2001 was also predicted. It is a different matter that the Court did not oblige them though it made me sad not because the Court dismissed my IA but because no reasons were given why a constitutional mandate, not yet quashed by any court, could not be acted upon. However, the subsequent events showed that all the hopes of such vested interest were completely belied.

With such difficult challenges confronting the Commission even before the actual election process could begin, there was a sense of nervousness bordering on despondency among the officers and staff under the District Administration when the Governor, on the recommendation of the Commission, issued notification for election to the three-tier Panchayat Institutions in the beginning of February 2001. This nervousness was mostly due to absence of any preparedness on the part of the District Administration for the inevitable. Therefore, the notification issued by the Governor for the conduct of election was taken with a sense of disbelief and fear in the minds of the District Magistrates and the BDOs to which I will come later. I will also explain how the Commission could overcome the problems as the election process started.

5

The Task Ahead—Election

As stated earlier, the Commission has a small manpower base in its office with only three officers from the State Civil Service to assist the Commissioner. However, in terms of the provisions in the Constitution and the Act the entire district administration as also the officers and staff of various departments of the government who are posted in the field are at the disposal of the Commission for the election. The administrative machinery has a long experience of more than 50 years in conducting elections to the State Legislature and the Parliament and, therefore, these officers and staff are mentally tuned to respond and take up any work relating to election as and when they are called upon by the district administration even at short notice. Therefore, the Commission did not face any problem in utilizing the services of the District Magistrates and other officers and staff posted in the district in completing the election process.

The State government also extended its full cooperation to the Commission in the conduct of the election, though occasionally it created some avoidable minor hurdles. Since elections were being held after a gap of 23 years and for the first time under a new legal frame consequent upon the 73rd amendment to the Constitution, the State government also did not take any chance. Moreover, as indicated earlier, the Patna High Court was monitoring continuously the steps being taken by the State government for the early conduct of election to the Panchayats. The Commission also involved the Divisional Commissioners who are the controlling authorities of the District Magistrates in the election process and it took no time for the officers to realize that the Commission meant business and once the election process was set in motion the entire field administration became fully active with the result that the election process was completed without much difficulties.

Initially the district administration was sceptical about holding elections to the Panchayats. However, once it became apparent that election to the Panchayats was a reality the entire field administration, both civil and police, did their job well and the co-ordination between the District Magistrates and the Superintendents of Police evident during the election process was commendable. It was because of such effective co-ordination between the civil and police administration that there was virtually no incident of violence near the polling station and the poll related violence was insignificant compared to the likely scale of violence anticipated by the media and the so-called well informed people. How this was possible will be explained later. At this stage it is necessary to refer to certain avoidable trivial hurdles created by the government which generated some mistrust in the Commission.

I have greatly appreciated the role played by the entire district administration and the Police Headquarters in the conduct of election to the Panchayats complying with the directions of the Commission in letter and spirit. Apart from the discipline of the service, the field officers became very alert after certain initial actions taken by the Commission to which I will revert shortly. The role of the Commission becomes very crucial with the process of filing nominations by the contesting candidates. The importance of nominations in the entire election process can hardly be overemphasized. During the process of filing nomination, its scrutiny and final acceptance by the Returning Officers the Commission got a number of complaints against the Returning Officers who allegedly rejected nominations which were otherwise valid. In selected cases it was found that the Returning Officers rejected nomination papers without any valid grounds thereby preventing eligible candidates from contesting. In some cases a particular candidate was shown as the only contesting candidate thereby making him/her eligible for getting elected unopposed but the Returning Officer separately prepared the final list of valid candidates for the same post making it a contested election but without the knowledge of the candidate shown unopposed winner due to which he never did any canvassing. Since the Commission had no power to review the decision of the Returning Officers except cancelling the election, the Commission recommended immediate transfer of the concerned Returning Officer to the government. There were few such cases where the Returning Officers had shown a distinct bias against or in favour of certain candidates. The Commission recommended immediate transfer and departmental proceedings against such erring officers. Government did not act on such recommendations of the Commission. It did not appreciate the fact that acceptance of the recommendation of a constitutional body would not only enhance the dignity of the Commission but would also enhance the image of the government itself in the eyes of the general public. In some cases the government transferred such officers but after a long gap of more than one month. During election it is promptness of the action which is more important than the quality of action. Election is conducted on war footing and there is no role for giving any predominance to the "ego". The indifferent attitude of the government on the recommendations of the Commission for departmental proceedings against the erring officers was not clear.

As against the indifferent attitude of the government to the recommendation of the Commission against certain officers, government showed undue haste in sending proposals to the Commission for approval for transferring certain district level senior officers for what is called administrative reasons. At least two secretaries to the government had met me after midnight in my Circuit House Room seeking my approval on the proposal of the State government to transfer certain officers from a particular district the next morning. I readily agreed to the proposal as

I believe that government is the ultimate authority to decide if certain District Magistrate or SP should be allowed to continue at a particular place in the interest of law and order. In this particular case any rigid approach on my part in the name of election would not have been a pragmatic one and, therefore, I had no hesitation in accepting the proposal of the State government. Unfortunately, the government did not reciprocate similarly only for a limited period of about two to three months for the conduct of election which should not only be free and fair but must also appear to be so.

In fact, the State government, though not publicly, have questioned the authority of the Commission to direct the government to transfer an officer or to initiate disciplinary action against a delinquent officer or even to debar an officer from election duty. A very reliable and senior officer, who was privy to certain deliberations in a meeting, told me that some senior Cabinet ministers had questioned the legal power of the Commission to enforce a code of conduct. However, it was only when the ministers were told that the powers and duties of the State Election Commission under Article 243-K of the Constitution are similar to the powers and duties of the Election Commission of India under Article 324 of the Constitution that the ministers accepted, reluctantly though, the independent constitutional status of the State Election Commission but not before ruing the decision of the government to appoint somebody to the post of State Election Commissioner who could not be of any help to them. Whatever be the reasons, willy nilly the political leadership of the ruling clan came to terms with the reality, grudgingly no doubt, that the dictates of the Commission on election matters had to be honoured. Another reason why the political executives could not muster enough courage to rub me on the wrong side was that by now, through certain initial actions taken by me, I made it amply clear that if I were not allowed to function independently and if there would be any hindrance in the discharge of my duties, I would postpone the election indefinitely or even cancel the election process though such an extreme steps (cancellation of election) would be very much to their liking, but they would not like to be seen as forcing me to take such an extreme step. Apparently the tough measures taken by a former Chief Election Commissioner of India still haunted the political executives and eventually they seemed to reconcile to the fact that the Commission would have to be allowed a free hand. Some senior political executives, including their top boss, had missed no opportunity to tauntingly equate me with a former Chief Election Commissioner of India and sarcastically commented that I also wanted to be a "hero" like Seshan. I had never exhibited any such propensity but definitely I am grateful to the political executives that their enforced good sense allowed me to conduct the two elections in my own way. Not a bad success, one would tend to presume.

With such unhelpful attitude of the government, which was otherwise co-operative in the conduct of election, on such crucial matter involving serious lapses on the part of the Returning Officers, the Commission had no option but to take recourse to the most unorthodox method of tackling such delinquent and recalcitrant officers by cancelling the election of the particular ward or Panchayat. Once the election process starts, it would be rarest of the rare occasions to cancel the same. In certain cases, no doubt, I had to cancel election and my order of cancellation was upheld by the High Court also. Therefore, I decided that the Returning Officers or any other officers involved in election related work who were found to be unfit for ensuring a free and fair election should be debarred from election related work. The Commission accordingly issued orders blacklisting a few Returning Officers and debarring them from election work. Such decisions of the Commission were given wide publicity by the print media which not only demoralized the concerned officers, but also had a deterrent effect on the entire election machinery. They realized the humiliation of being debarred from election related work and how this could also be used by the government against such officers in future.

In fact, the government's reluctance to act on the recommendation of the Commission against certain officers continued till election to the municipalities after one year in April-June, 2002. During election to the Panchayats it was noticed that seven District Magistrates and two Divisional Commissioners (not the two Commissioners who were temporarily debarred referred to later in this chapter) were not upto the mark and accordingly after the election to the Panchayats was over the Commission recommended the transfer of these seven District Magistrates and two Divisional Commissioners. Government transferred the two Divisional Commissioners and five of the seven District Magistrates. The government remained silent on the transfer of the remaining two officers and in the meantime by-election to the Panchayats was announced and the poll was to take place during January, 2002. I refused to conduct by-poll in the two districts whose District Magistrates were not transferred by the government. I got frantic telephonic requests from the Secretary of the concerned department that by-election could be held in January, 2002 and government would ensure the transfer of these two District Magistrates immediately thereafter. I did not agree and the government allowed these two District Magistrates to play truant. The two District Magistrates proceeded on leave before the election process started but immediately after the election process was over the two officers were allowed to join their old posts. In the meantime notification for election to the municipalities had to be issued in February, 2002. I refused to conduct election to the municipalities falling within the two districts whose District Magistrates had not been transferred as per the recommendations of the Commission. The notification was issued but the municipalities of these two districts were excluded. This was again highlighted by the print media and apparently to avoid any embarrassment, the government finally transferred those two District Magistrates. But I refused to take any further action unless the successor District Magistrates joined their posts. Thus after the two new District Magistrates took over, separate notification for election to the municipalities in those two districts was also issued.

All the seven affected District Magistrates filed writ petitions in the Patna High Court challenging the authority of the Commission to recommend their transfer. They also contended that no show cause notice had been issued to them before their transfer. The Commission took the plea in the High Court that under the provisions of the Constitution and the Act it was the prerogative of the Commission to engage any officer in election duty and accordingly the Commission could disengage such officer if it is found that it would not be possible to conduct free and fair election through such officers. Since the recommendation was not the result of departmental proceedings there was no question of calling for an explanation from the concerned officer. It is a sad reflection on the officers holding such important post as District Magistrates to be so ill-informed about the jurisdiction of the Commission. Government remained neutral in the court while a simple statement by the government that the Commission has the constitutional authority to requisition and consequently to de-requisition the services of any officer and staff for the conduct of election could have been enough for the court to decide such writ petitions. However, it is satisfying to note that the High Court appreciated the Commission's stand. But one of the District Magistrates moved a petition before the Central Administrative Tribunal against his transfer.

There was yet another case I should refer to at this stage as it also had a bearing on the conduct of election. Though I joined on September 26, 2000, I could get the officers and staff as per the sanctioned strength some time in the middle of December, 2000. The only Deputy Secretary posted in the Commission was also transferred to the newly-created State of Jharkhand from November 15, 2000. As a result there was no officer below me to sign even a routine order passed by the Commission.

As stated earlier, the Commission had, in the past, completed the preliminary work including printing of ballot papers for the Panchayat election scheduled during the first half of 1996. The voters list was also made up-to-date. The list of polling stations was finalized and approved by the Commission which also identified the reserved constituencies and approved the same. However, on account of the judgment and order passed by the Patna High Court on March 19,1996, election got deferred as the State government filed a SLP in the Supreme Court which was pending decision. The Patna High Court had quashed certain sections of the Act relating to reservation for the posts of Chairpersons of the Panchayats as also for election of Judicial Panchayats. In the circumstances, the Commission initiated the process of election in October, 2000, assuming that the main preparatory work prior to filing nominations for the election was complete and that voters list, identification of polling stations, reservation of constituencies etc. would not require any modification. The Commission would only be required to get the ballot papers printed afresh as the ones printed earlier by the Commission were outdated without the names of the contesting candidates and certain other essential details. Thus the only major time-consuming work was to get the ballot papers printed before deciding the poll schedule.

Going by my overall assessment about the administration I thought it prudent to have a direct interaction with the District Magistrates and the Divisional Commissioners to obtain an idea about the state of preparedness of the district administration for the conduct of election. Accordingly, a meeting of all the District Magistrates and Divisional Commissioners was called on January 16, 2001. At the end of the meeting I was shocked to realise that the district administration was not mentally prepared for the election and that the District Magistrates still had doubts about the prospect of the election. By that time it was too late for the Commission to take a different view. Accordingly, I made it very clear to the District Magistrates and the Divisional Commissioners that the Commission meant business and anybody entertaining any hopes to the contrary would do so at his own risk. But the question bothering me was how to make the District Magistrates realize my seriousness. Absence of two Divisional Commissioners, one of whom is a senior officer and about whom I have always had good opinion, made my job very easy. Immediately after the meeting I announced that two absentee Divisional Commissioners would be debarred from election related work for not attending the meeting called by the Commission. This was given wide publicity by the print media and it worked like a miracle. Though it was quite humiliating for the two Divisional Commissioners, I had no other option left to make my intention clear. Moreover, I believe in taking only one or two actions which would correct the whole system going by the maxim "that country is governed best which governs the least" as the guiding principle for any administrator. The 16 January meeting was a turning point and it was amazing to see how the lacklustre attitude of the district administration changed overnight and the initiatives the district administration took from that day onward were commendable. District Magistrates on their own went on submitting proposals for changing location of polling stations on grounds that the old locations were not convenient for the voters specially for those belonging to the weaker section. Such *suo motu* action of the District Election officers only indicated that they had earlier not done their ground work properly presuming that election would not take place.

My problems were far from over. With the filing of nomination papers there was a clear realization that election to the Panchayats was a reality, initial scepticism notwithstanding. Some politically alert people soon came to know that names of many eligible persons were missing from the voters lists. This led to the filing of large number of writs in the Patna High Court seeking revision of relevant voters lists before elections. By then it was too late and as per provisions of the Act no change in the voters list is permissible after the issue of notification by the Governor. I informed the court accordingly which was accepted. But all of a sudden a different single Bench of the court took the view that it would be illegal to deny the right of franchise to an otherwise eligible person. I was summoned by the Court to explain the difficulties if the writ petitions were allowed resulting in the revision of the voters lists. I explained the above legal provisions against such revisions and also that inclusion of names in the electoral roll at that stage would complicate the matter as once included as voter the person concerned would automatically acquire the right of filing nomination for a particular post which could not be allowed then. Moreover, if allowed, this had to be permitted in all such cases throughout the State. The Court was not convinced observing that it would give only voting right to a newly enrolled person and no other right. To this my reply was that such a "truncated" voter would not be legally sound. I also made it clear that if due to revision of the electoral roll at a late stage the election process gets derailed I should not be held responsible. The judgement was reserved and after about two weeks the Court mandated that wherever in any particular electoral roll names of 100 or more eligible persons were found missing the same should be revised before holding the election. It was totally frustrating me as it might lead to revision of voters' lists *de novo* in many constituencies throughout the State. I was at a loss. I had no option but to file a Letter Patent Appeal (LPA) before a Double Bench against the order of the Single Bench. My argument was that the figure of 100 was arbitrary as the number of persons could not be a determining factor in deciding a particular electoral roll as valid or invalid. Further, as per the Supreme Court decision in the past once the election process starts judicial intervention is not permissible unless it is for furthering the progress of the process and not otherwise, besides the specific legal provisions in the Act referred to above against such revision of voters lists. To my great relief the LPA was allowed by the Court and this effectively sealed the fate of all such writs.

I have narrated these experiences just to emphasize the hurdles I had to cross and the steps I had to take to establish the authority of the Commission. I must appreciate that the district administration, the main arm of the Commission in the conduct of election, did everything possible to establish the identity and credibility of the body and the entire election process passed off almost with clock-work precision. Thus if I have faced big challenges right from the beginning, I have also been able to overcome these. I must give full credit to the district administration, both civil and police, for making the presence of the Commission felt. As far as the Commission is concerned my officers and the staff in the Commission followed my principle that the presence of the Commission should not be seen but felt. The district administration including police administration proved beyond doubt that if the final authority issues unambiguous directions and the authority takes full responsibility, the district administration would not lag behind in proving their worth. The district administration proved this in ample manner during the two general elections, one to the Panchayats during April-May, 2001 and the other to the municipalities during April-June, 2002, i.e., two general elections within a period of about one year.

At a time when the general atmosphere in the State was not conducive to the holding of elections due to government's lack of interest in the poll and the print media's apprehension about the likely violence it became very difficult for the Commission to decide on a poll schedule sufficiently in advance. The State government decided that election to all the four posts, i.e., Mukhiya of Gram Panchayat, member of Gram Panchayat, member of Panchayat Samiti and member of Zila Parishad, would be held simultaneously. The elections to these four posts are direct, i.e., these posts are filled up directly by the voters of their respective territorial constituencies (wards). There are 8,471 posts of Mukhiya of Gram Panchayats, 1,16,029 posts of member of Gram Panchayats, 11,611 posts of member of Panchayat Samitis and 1,162 members of the Zila Parishads, making a total of 1,37,273 posts for which direct election was to be held. Table 5.1 and Table 5.2 will give an idea about the volume of work involved.

Table 5.1: District-wise Basic Data

Sl. No.	District	No. of Blocks	No. of Polling Stations	Gram Panchayat Mukhiya		Member of Gram Panchayat	
				No. of Posts	No. of Candidates	No. of Posts	No. of Candidates
1.	Patna	23	4558	334	4960	4558	10553
2.	Rohtas	19	3342	244	4346	3342	7818
3.	Bhojpur	14	3114	228	3774	3114	6539
4.	Nalanda	20	3400	249	3737	3400	6704
5.	Buxar	11	1980	142	2311	1980	4194
6.	Kaimur	11	1902	153	2555	1902	3560
7.	Gaya	24	4602	333	4661	4602	8958
8.	Nawada	14	2527	187	2318	2527	4504
9.	Aurangabad	11	2837	203	3444	2837	5553
10.	Jehanabad	12	2206	161	2510	2206	4914
11.	Saran	20	4684	330	4483	4684	10585
12.	Siwan	16	4086	293	2937	4086	7221
13.	Gopalganj	14	3193	235	2479	3193	5535
14.	Muzaffarpur	16	5352	387	4538	5352	11959
15.	Vaishali	16	4013	290	3640	4013	10549
16.	E. Champaran	27	5686	410	3411	5686	13073
17.	W. Champaran	18	4219	319	3928	4219	9319
18.	Sitamarhi	17	3837	273	3050	3837	8441
19.	Seohar	5	747	53	667	747	1360
20.	Bhagalpur	16	3128	242	2819	3128	6121
21.	Banka	11	2481	185	2406	2481	4451
22.	Madhubani	20	5516	399	4755	5516	9328
23.	Samastipur	20	5212	381	4596	5212	11895
24.	Darbhanga	18	4570	329	3483	4570	8145
25.	Saharsa	10	2104	153	1771	2104	4833
26.	Madhepura	13	2242	170	2271	2242	4751
27.	Supaul	11	2529	180	2356	2529	5388
28.	Purnia	14	3426	251	3087	3426	6473
29.	Araria	9	2992	218	2849	2992	5974
30.	Kishanganj	7	1769	126	1530	1769	4234
31.	Katihar	16	3273	239	3162	3273	5385
32.	Munger	9	1363	101	1313	1363	2678
33.	Jamui	10	1963	153	1979	1963	3684
34.	Begusarai	18	3490	257	2734	3490	8158
35.	Khagaria	7	1859	129	1672	1859	4559
36.	Lakhisarai	6	1115	80	1008	1115	1833
37.	Shekhpura	6	712	54	490	712	1221
	Total	529	116029	8471	108030	116029	240450

Table 5.1 (*Continued*)

Sl. No.	*District*	*No. of Blocks*	*No. of Polling Stations*	*Member of Panchayat Samiti*		*Member of Zila Parishad*	
				No. of Posts	*No. of Candidates*	*No. of Posts*	*No. of Candidates*
1.	Patna	23	4558	454	3066	46	786
2.	Rohtas	19	3342	330	2500	33	586
3.	Bhojpur	14	3114	310	2108	31	467
4.	Nalanda	20	3400	342	2114	34	594
5.	Buxar	11	1980	200	1520	20	373
6.	Kaimur	11	1902	192	1383	19	377
7.	Gaya	24	4602	460	2763	46	626
8.	Nawada	14	2527	254	1368	25	258
9.	Aurangabad	11	2837	285	1893	28	426
10.	Jehanabad	12	2206	222	1584	22	362
11.	Saran	20	4684	469	3056	47	392
12.	Siwan	16	4086	411	2114	41	340
13.	Gopalganj	14	3193	322	1669	32	292
14.	Muzaffarpur	16	5352	535	3036	54	592
15.	Vaishali	16	4013	399	2484	41	584
16.	E. Champaran	27	5686	571	3454	57	644
17.	W. Champaran	18	4219	421	2709	42	457
18.	Sitamarhi	17	3837	384	2243	38	451
19.	Seohar	5	747	72	367	7	1573
20.	Bhagalpur	16	3128	314	1752	31	396
21.	Banka	11	2481	250	1476	25	252
22.	Madhubani	20	5516	545	2981	56	569
23.	Samastipur	20	5212	522	3124	51	599
24.	Darbhanga	18	4570	459	2530	47	470
25.	Saharsa	10	2104	209	1282	21	257
26.	Madhepura	13	2242	225	1436	23	248
27.	Supaul	11	2529	255	1463	25	289
28.	Purnia	14	3426	346	1767	34	310
29.	Araria	9	2992	303	1722	30	271
30.	Kishanganj	7	1769	176	1088	18	144
31.	Katihar	16	3273	329	1868	33	325
32.	Munger	9	1363	136	816	14	192
33.	Jamui	10	1963	193	1212	20	223
34.	Begusarai	18	3490	348	1984	35	424
35.	Khagaria	7	1859	185	1271	18	255
36.	Lakhisarai	6	1115	113	586	11	138
37.	Shekhpura	6	712	70	313	7	58
	Total	529	116029	11611	70102	1162	15600

Table 5.2: Post-wise Number of Candidates

Sl. No.	District	*GPS	*GPM	*PSS	*ZPS	Total
1.	Patna	10553	4960	3066	786	19365
2.	Rohtas	7818	4346	2500	586	15250
3.	Bhojpur	6539	3774	2108	467	12888
4.	Nalanda	6704	3737	2114	594	13149
5.	Buxar	4194	2311	1520	373	8398
6.	Kaimur	3560	2555	1383	377	7875
7.	Gaya	8958	4661	2763	626	17008
8.	Nawada	4504	2318	1368	258	8448
9.	Aurangabad	5553	3444	1893	426	11316
10.	Jehanabad	4914	2510	1584	362	9370
11.	Saran	10585	4483	3056	392	18516
12.	Siwan	7221	2937	2114	340	12612
13.	Gopalganj	5535	2479	1669	292	9975
14.	Muzaffarpur	11959	4538	3036	592	20125
15.	Vaishali	10549	3640	2484	584	17257
16.	E. Champaran	13073	3411	3454	644	22582
17.	W. Champaran	9319	3928	2709	457	16413
18.	Sitamarhi	8441	3050	2243	451	14185
19.	Sheohar	1360	667	367	1573	3967
20.	Bhagalpur	6121	2819	1752	396	11088
21.	Banka	4451	2406	1476	252	8585
22.	Madhubani	9328	4755	2981	569	17633
23.	Samastipur	11895	4596	3124	599	20214
24.	Darbhanga	8145	3483	2530	470	14628
25.	Saharsa	4833	1771	1282	257	8143
26.	Madhepura	4751	2271	1436	248	8706
27.	Supaul	5388	2356	1463	289	9496
28.	Purnia	6473	3087	1767	310	11637
29.	Araria	5974	2849	1722	271	10816
30.	Kishanganj	4234	1530	1088	144	6996
31.	Katihar	5385	3162	1868	325	10740
32.	Munger	2678	1313	816	192	4999
33.	Jamui	3684	1979	1212	223	7148
34.	Begusarai	8158	2734	1984	424	13300
35.	Khagaria	4559	1672	1271	255	7757
36.	Lakhisarai	1833	1008	586	138	3565
37.	Shekhpura	1221	490	313	58	2082
	Total	240450	108030	70102	15600	436232

* GPS—Gram Panchayat Member PSS—Panchayat Samiti Member
GPM—Gram Panchayat Mukhiya ZPS—Zila Parishad Member

The Commission was in favour of completing the poll on one single day throughout the State. The rationale of such a view was that single day polling would keep miscreants and the anti-social elements confined to their limited areas of influence and would not provide them enough opportunity to create any mischief in other areas which were not prone to disturbance. Moreover, unlike election to the State Legislature and Parliament when one constituency would have a large number of polling stations spread over a vast area, more than 90 per cent of the 1,37,273 posts of the Panchayat would mean one polling station for one ward, i.e., every ward of a Gram Panchayat member would have only one polling station which will be mostly located within the *mohalla* (locality) and very close to the residences of the voters whose number will be between 300 and 400. Since in such a *mohalla* people are familiar with each other, the miscreants would find it difficult to create trouble. But since the assessment of the likely law and order problem was that there would be more violence and blood-shed than what was witnessed during the election in 1978 (when reportedly more than 700 people were killed) the State government was reluctant to accept my proposal about one day poll throughout the State. The State was not hopeful of getting any additional security force from other States and from the Central government and, therefore, the government was left only with its own police force and the homeguards for deployment during the election. The State government, therefore, was of the view that the election should be conducted in phases, not exceeding six in all.

The most important reason for conducting election in phases was that the District Magistrate would be in a position to do the job with the manpower available within the district and under his control.

The Commission had no option as the State government is the most competent authority to assess the likely law and order situation. Accordingly, on the recommendation of the

Commission the Governor issued notification on February 7, 2001 for election for the first phase and for sixth phase on February 22, 2001. The dates for poll in different phases were fixed, April 11, 2001 for the first phase and April 30, 2001 for the sixth phase. Counting of votes was to be done on May 5, 2001. The entire election process took more than three months to be completed.

The schedule for filing nomination, scrutiny of nomination etc. and date of poll for different phases was announced in due course by the Commission. The response of the people in the rural areas specially women was unbelievable. People came out in large numbers to file nominations. Newspaper reports suggested that almost a festival like atmosphere prevailed in the rural areas and in certain places the candidates came in big processions on elephants with band party etc. to file nominations. There was general belief, which looked more imaginary than real, that a Gram Panchayat would get an annual grant of between Rs. three million and Rs. five million which would be spent under the control of the Mukhiya for the development of the Panchayat. This belief led to filing of nomination for the post of Mukhiya in large numbers followed by nomination for the post of member of Zila Parishad with an eye on the post of Chairperson of the Zila Parishad election for which was indirect.

As stated earlier, elections to all the four posts were to be held simultaneously. The Commission assessed that about 200 million ballot papers would have to be printed. This number, however, got reduced to about 180 million after taking into account the cases of uncontested election *vide* Table 5.3, mostly for the post of member of Gram Panchayat. Since there are four different posts, four different ballot papers were to be printed. This made the job more complicated and here also the Commission faced some avoidable obstacles created by government which allowed very limited time to get the ballot papers printed in advance of the poll. I would shortly refer to the complexity of the problems and also the response thereto by all concerned.

Table 5.3: Members Elected Uncontested

Sl. No.	*District*	**GPS*	**GPM*	**PSS*	**ZPS*	*Total*
1.	Patna	-	-	-	-	-
2.	Rohtas	720	-	-	-	720
3.	Bhojpur	594	-	2	-	596
4.	Nalanda	-	-	-	-	0
5.	Buxar	445	1	1	-	447
6.	Kaimur	519	-	3	-	522
7.	Gaya	1388	2	27	0	1417
8.	Nawada	-	-	-	-	0
9.	Aurangabad	808	-	4	-	812
10.	Jehanabad	523	-	1	-	524
11.	Saran	-	-	-	-	0
12.	Siwan	1287	3	-	-	1290
13.	Gopalganj	1008	4	12	-	1024
14.	Muzaffarpur	-	-	-	-	0
15.	Vaishali	672	1	2	-	675
16.	E. Champaran	1244	1	18	-	1263
17.	W. Champaran	-	-	-	-	0
18.	Sitamarhi	-	-	-	-	0
19.	Sheohar	232	-	3	-	235
20.	Bhagalpur	846	2	17	-	865
21.	Banka	819	-	11	-	830
22.	Madhubani	1824	1	16	-	1841
23.	Samastipur	1148	1	9	-	1158
24.	Darbhanga	1114	2	15	-	1131
25.	Saharsa	538	2	4	1	545
26.	Madhepura	602	-	3	-	605
27.	Supaul	641	3	-	-	644
28.	Purnia	1115	7	24	-	1146
29.	Araria	545	-	12	-	557
30.	Kishanganj	303	-	4	-	307
31.	Katihar	820	-	12	-	832
32.	Munger	-	-	-	-	0
33.	Jamui	597	-	5	-	602
34.	Begusarai	654	1	6	-	661
35.	Khagaria	383	-	2	-	385
36.	Lakhisarai	287	-	1	1	289
37.	Shekhpura	239	1	5	-	245
	Total	21915	32	219	2	22,168

* GPS—Gram Panchayat Member PSS—Panchayat Samiti Member
GPM—Gram Panchayat Mukhiya ZPS—Zila Parishad Member

Since the Commission did not have any previous experience of conducting election I did not agree to take the responsibility of getting the ballot papers printed. The main reason behind my decision not to get the ballot paper printed was that even though the District Election officers were capable and were also ready to print ballot papers locally, the State government at the decision making level did not favour it fearing that in the process many District Magistrates might get involved in unnecessary controversy. Under the circumstances, I suggested that the State government, i.e., the Department of Panchayati Raj, should take the responsibility of getting the ballot papers printed and the Commission would extend all possible assistance. This was agreed upon and thence the long drawn process started.

As I have stated earlier, the Commission in the past got the ballot papers printed for the election originally scheduled in the first half of 1996. These ballot papers did not have the names of the candidates printed thereon and it was thought that the names would be written by the polling party after reaching the polling station. I was horrified as it was physically impossible for a particular polling party to write down the names of all the contesting candidates for four different posts on about 400 ballot papers for each category of post. That is, writing the names of candidates numbering between two for member of Gram Panchayat and 35 for the post of Mukhiya was not physically possible besides the likely apprehension that the polling party would be exposed to anti-social elements. Further, the ballot papers were printed in the beginning of 1996 and they remained in store for five years making their usefulness suspect. I, therefore, refused to accept those ballot papers.

I decided that the ballot papers should be printed afresh with the names of the contesting candidates, their election symbols, series number and serial number of each ballot paper, name of the District, Block, Panchayat and the ward number with counterfoil of each ballot paper as in the case of election to the State Legislature and to Parliament. I got a very amusing suggestion from the government that the Commission could utilize part of the old ballot papers which were usable. I could not believe as how such a suggestion could be made as those ballot papers had only the election symbols printed in random while the election symbols were to be allotted to the contesting candidates in a manner to be prescribed by the Commission and it was preposterous to think that it would be in accordance with the order in which the election symbols were printed in the ballot papers. I bluntly refused to entertain such suggestion.

The administrative department accordingly initiated the process of selecting a suitable printing press for printing the ballot papers. Since the two State government printing presses expressed their inability to print the ballot papers, the administrative department selected the printing press of a neighbouring State Government Undertaking which also prints many documents including budget papers of the Bihar Government. Since it was a State Government Undertaking and a Security Press it was considered appropriate to get the job done by the above Press and the decision of the administrative department of the government could not be faulted. However, during the inter-department consultation one department suggested that the administrative department should also get quotation from other State government Printing Presses before taking any final decision. This was an impractical suggestion as the cost and the logistics of getting the ballot papers printed at far off places would not permit such a futile exercise as that would totally derail the election schedule. The administrative department remained firm on its earlier decision. But this did not deter the concerned department again from raising doubt. It is understood that the department took the line that it would be suicidal to get the ballot papers printed from one source. It did not appreciate the fact that procuring the ballot papers from multiple sources would create a lot of administrative problems. I must give credit to the administrative department for overruling such apprehension.

While the process of selecting a suitable printing press was going on, the Commission came across certain legal problems. Although the Act and the Rules are quite comprehensive, in the absence of any election in the past the Commission had no idea about any practical difficulties that could crop up all of a sudden. A particular rule provides for elaborate specifications about the form and design of a ballot paper. Since the people of the State are quite litigant I could visualize that it might not be possible to adhere to such elaborate specifications and if there would be any deviation, even a very minor technical one, the whole election process could be in jeopardy. There was another rule which makes it obligatory to place three ballot boxes at a time for different posts in each polling station for putting the ballot papers therein by every voter after marking his/her preference. It was unfeasible as to how a voter would be in a position to distinguish different ballot boxes for different posts and one could imagine the confusion in the voting compartment besides the time taken by each voter. Since the provisions were there in the rule I had no option to act otherwise. I, therefore, suggested amendment to each of the above two rules according to which the Commission was to be given the omnibus power to select the form and design of a ballot paper and also to decide the number of ballot boxes to be used at a time in a polling station. The government amended the rules in the shortest possible time which made my job much easier.

It seemed that the problem with the ballot papers was never-ending. It occurred to me that the majority of the voters who are illiterate, specially the women voters would find it extremely difficult to distinguish ballot paper for one category of post from the ballot papers of other categories of posts unless there could be something eye-catching. Since the polling station would be mostly within the walking distance of every voter a large turn-out of voters was anticipated and, therefore, any confusion on account of the ballot papers would delay the voting process abnormally. I, therefore, decided that the ballot papers for each of the four posts should be printed in four different and distinct colours which could be easily identified by the voters. This was easier said than done as the printing press expressed its difficulty in getting papers of different colours in such short time. I then decided that the press could use off-white paper as the base and the names of the candidates, shaded portion, serial number and other printed materials could be in different colours, like, green, red etc. keeping black printing materials for ballot papers meant for the post of member of Gram Panchayat due to some technical reasons associated with printing machines. The printing press found my suggestion practical and readily accepted it. The Commission gave wide publicity through newspaper advertisements about the colours of the ballot papers for different posts. There were rare mistakes committed by the voters in casting their votes for the candidates of their choice for different posts and putting all the four ballot papers individually folded in one ballot box. A specimen of the ballot paper is at Appendix-A.

As per the rules the names of the candidates whose nominations were finally accepted after withdrawal were to be written in alphabetical order in Devnagari script on the ballot paper and for that purpose their names were to be first written in Form-9 as prescribed under the rule. Though the staff engaged for writing the names of the contesting candidates alphabetically have the requisite knowledge about Devnagari script the sheer number of contesting candidates made their job extremely difficult. The number of valid contesting candidates was 4,36,232 *vide* Table 5.2 and one could imagine the magnitude of the total work to be done by the staff in a very short time. To follow the alphabetical order till the last letter of the name would mean a very strenuous process. I, therefore, decided that we should go by alphabets of first name only and accordingly requisition in Form-9 was sent to the printing press. To make sure that there was no mistake some senior people were deputed to scrutinize the alphabetical orders in Form-9. These senior staff tried to prove their expertise and in the process some changes were suggested in the alphabetical order without realizing that any change in the alphabetical order of the names without corresponding change in the allotted election symbols would make the ballot papers invalid. When the matter was brought to my notice I immediately decided that there would be no change in the alphabetical order as shown in Form-9 by the Returning Officer even if it was not accurate.

Though the Returning Officers did their best to ensure that there was no mistake in the finally printed ballot papers and senior officers from the Commission and the government also supervised the work personally in the printing press certain mistakes took place inadvertently which was again on account of the sheer volume of work and the limited time available. Since the printing was computerized, any error in feeding the input would bring out wrongly printed ballot papers. It mostly happened in printing election symbols against the candidates which were not as per Form-9. Such mistakes were detected at the time of dispatching the ballot papers to the polling stations and wherever the Returning Officer was alert he could get the ballot papers reprinted in time and this was possible because the printing press was at convenient location and distance. Nevertheless, certain cases of wrongly printed ballot papers could not be detected and in such cases election was cancelled and in due course repoll ordered.

I have perhaps allotted more space than required to focus on the problems associated with the printing of ballot papers. I have done so to highlight the magnitude and complexity of the problem for conducting election simultaneously for four different categories of posts in the Panchayat system. In retrospect, I could see that the public in general and the voters in particular found the entire election process very smooth and easy to follow.

Elections were held as per schedule and repoll became necessary in 3,623 polling stations out of the total number of polling stations of 1,16,029 *vide* Table 5.4 and one should agree that percentage-wise it was not a very high figure and considering the fact that it was altogether a new exercise after a gap of 23 years by an inexperienced election machinery. Moreover, in a large number of cases repoll became necessary as the ballot papers were wrongly printed and this mistake could not be detected in time. In some cases repoll became necessary due to the mischief created by certain anti-social elements by putting liquid coloured materials on the polled ballot papers specially on the first day which prompted the polling personnel to withdraw immediately thinking that their worst fear of violence was to be there any moment. That such fear was misplaced would be explained later.

Table 5.4: No. of Polling Stations where repoll held

Sl. No.	*District*	*1st Phase 11.4.01*	*2nd Phase 15.4.01*	*3rd Phase 19.4.01*	*4th Phase 23.4.01*	*5th Phase 27.4.01*	*6th Phase 30.4.01*	*Total*
1.	Patna	63	95	14	7	5	86	270
2.	Rohtas	38	17	20	10	12	9	106
3.	Bhojpur	8	6	1	-	-	2	17
4.	Nalanda	12	5	32	4	-	-	53
5.	Buxar	23	-	16	14	-	-	53
6.	Kaimur	3	41	11	-	14	-	69
7.	Gaya	27	8	13	10	11	16	85
8.	Nawada	107	73	17	4	-	1	202
9.	Aurangabad	30	22	10	2	10	27	101
10.	Jehanabad	10	9	3	4	3	6	35
11.	Saran	67	59	83	15	8	39	271
12.	Siwan	74	12	19	-	-	-	105
13.	Gopalganj	45	39	66	22	17	25	214
14.	Muzaffarpur	88	43	40	120	23	24	338
15.	Vaishali	37	48	19	18	3	-	125
16.	E. Champaran	154	158	47	35	-	-	394
17.	W. Champaran	7	-	14	8	1	-	30
18.	Sitamarhi	2	7	16	-	8	-	33
19.	Sheohar	2	3	-	-	-	-	5
20.	Bhagalpur	26	-	2	-	-	-	28
21.	Banka	16	25	1	2	-	-	44
22.	Madhubani	14	44	30	8	5	-	101
23.	Samastipur	146	-	-	14	-	5	165
24.	Darbhanga	10	17	1	1	4	7	40
25.	Saharsa	12	14	15	10	-	-	51
26.	Madhepura	10	26	35	104	2	6	183
27.	Supaul	102	1	5	12	-	-	120
28.	Purnia	6	55	10	-	-	15	86
29.	Araria	31	15	-	9	2	1	58
30.	Kishanganj	-	-	-	-	-	-	-
31.	Katihar	6	1	1	-	-	-	8
32.	Munger	5	-	-	-	-	11	16
33.	Jamui	17	8	6	6	22	22	81
34.	Begusarai	6	-	-	-	-	-	6
35.	Khagaria	4	9	1	-	-	-	14
36.	Lakhisarai	22	34	8	5	-	-	69
37.	Shekhpura	20	9	5	13	-	-	47
	Total	1250	903	561	457	150	302	3623

Counting of votes started after the repoll was over and with initial delay, the counting picked up gradually and it was completed at the earliest. Since the ballot papers were of different colours for different posts it was easy for the counting staff to segregate the ballot papers post-wise. Senior officers were deputed as counting supervisors and a Returning Officer could declare the result only after the same was approved by the supervisor deputed by the Commission.

While the counting process was going on the Commission was confronted with a peculiar problem where a decision was to be taken instantly. The three most significant decisions taken by the Commission during counting process are briefly narrated below.

In some cases polling was boycotted by the voters. I made a distinction between the boycott observed by the voters as a protest against the lapses on the part of the election machinery like delay in reaching ballot papers to the polling stations or sending ballot papers of one polling station to another polling station. In such cases I decided to hold repoll as the boycott by the voters was considered reasonable. However, where the voters boycotted election on their own on some perceived grievances the Commission took the view that number of votes cast in such polling station would be taken as "zero" and accordingly "+0" would be shown as polled by each contesting candidate and the results should be declared accordingly except that for the post of member of the Gram Panchayat repoll would be held as it was not feasible to declare the result based on that particular polling station representing one Gram Panchayat ward and in such cases by-poll was held later.

In another case booth capturing was evident and it was a clear case of rigging. Since such rigging either goes in favour or against a particular candidate the Commission presumed that the contesting candidates had a role in booth capturing and the polling agents of the contesting candidates became a party to the rigging process. Accordingly, I decided that voting in such polling station was to be treated as vitiated and the contesting candidates were shown as securing "zero" number of votes and accordingly results for all the posts except that of member of the concerned Gram Panchayat was declared and by-poll was held subsequently for the post of member of Gram Panchayat as explained in the preceding paragraph. The Commission took such a drastic step in these cases as otherwise it would amount to giving premium to the anti-social elements and also to the candidates who became a party to the rigging process either deliberately or due to their inaction.

The last significant decision was fixing the cut off percentage of voting for the purpose of seeking prior approval of the Commission before taking a decision about inclusion or otherwise of such votes in the final result sheet. The social system in the State was taken as relevant in deciding the cut off point. In the State the villages are generally inhabited by people belonging to a particular caste and in many cases each *mohalla* (locality) of a village is inhabited by people belonging to a particular caste and in usual course there is not much interaction between the people of different castes in their day to day life. Thus on the day of poll for election to the State Legislative Assembly and the Parliament the mobility of the voters gets restricted as voters of certain *mohalla* specially those inhabited by weaker section of the society would not either be allowed to go to the polling station or they on their own would not dare to go to polling station specially if the road to the polling station passes through a village or *mohalla* inhabited by people belonging to a different caste, to cast their votes. Since failure of such voters to cast their votes may go in favour of a particular candidate he would try to ensure that such voters are intimidated against going to the polling station. The situation in respect of election to the Panchayats is completely different as every polling station would have between 300 and 400 voters and the polling station would mostly be very close to their places of residence and, therefore, there would be no obstacle on their way to the polling station. Reservation of not less than one-third of the total seats for women besides reservation for the Scheduled Castes and the Scheduled Tribes also resulted in qualitative change in the rural areas as the presence of large number of candidates from the reserved category of persons, including women, encouraged the voters to come out in large numbers on the day of poll. In fact, the women voters in many cases outnumbered the male voters and it was almost a festival-like atmosphere in the rural areas with women coming in their colourful dresses with children braving the strong sun to cast their votes. This was widely reported by the print media and all the major television channels flashed the long queues of voters throughout the day. In fact, in some cases voting percentage almost touched 100. I, therefore, decided that it would be reasonable to fix 95 per cent as the cut-off point for any particular polling station. And if any polling station would record voting of more than 95 per cent either for one post or more than one post, the Returning Officer would obtain specific prior approval of the Commission for all the four posts before deciding if such votes would be included or not in the final result sheet. The Commission got many such cases and gave its decision instantly.

The above decisions of the Commission have been appreciated by all concerned. However some people questioned my last decision referred to above. Their argument was that why should prior approval of the Commission be necessary for such post/posts for which voting percentage was not more than 95 simply because there had been more than 95 per cent voting for, say, only one post. I dismissed such a plea. My reasoning was that if the voters had been intimidated for casting their votes even for one post, the atmosphere in the polling station would get vitiated and, therefore, the voters would not feel free to cast their votes in the particular polling station. One small drop of poison in a cup of milk makes the full cup of milk poisonous.

It will be relevant in this context to refer to a very unusual step, perhaps hitherto unheard of, taken by me in ensuring fair counting of votes in a particular district. The concerned District Magistrate was not only inefficient but also an extremely weak person. Before the start of counting process some reliable persons told me that certain criminal elements were trying to influence the District Magistrate in ensuring victory of certain candidates. I made some informal enquiry through official sources and it was confirmed that the allegations were correct. Counting was to start the next day. Immediately and without letting anybody know about the matter I telephonically requested the District Magistrate of a neighbouring district who had by then completed counting in his district to be in readiness with a contingent of officers and staff to take up some important assignment next morning. Similar request was made to the concerned Divisional Commissioner. I also authorized the Divisional Commissioner to mobilize any officers and staff in the four districts under his charge.

I issued an order making the Divisional Commissioner overall incharge for counting of votes in the particular district and authorized the District Magistrate of the neighbouring district referred to above to closely supervise the counting. The order was sent through fax followed by telephonic message late in the afternoon and the Divisional Commissioner and the District Magistrate of the neighbouring district moved with the required manpower and reached the particular district late evening to take up counting work next morning. This was hot news for the print media which gave it wide publicity in their morning edition. The counting was completed in the shortest possible time and without any complaint. However, newspaper reports suggested that there was an abortive attempt on the life of the Divisional Commissioner who was camping in the local government Circuit House. I was quite worried, as, in the event of any harm to the officer I would consider myself responsible since I took the unusual step of debarring the District Magistrate from counting work and entrusting the responsibility to the Divisional Commissioner. I was greatly relieved when the officer told me on telephone that he was fine. He also told me that he had moved with his own security force from the Divisional Headquarters as he doubted the competence of the security force of the district concerned.

The above step, no doubt, enhanced the impartial and effective role of the Commission but it was also fraught with grave consequences on the personal safety of the officers and staff imported from outside the district.

6

Ballots Versus Bullets

An election can be considered free and fair if the voters, whom Sir Winston Churchill has described as the "little man", have freely exercised their voting rights in favour of the candidates of their choice. If the "little man" has been intimidated in the exercise of his voting rights the election cannot be treated as free and fair. Therefore, the first and foremost requirement of a free and fair election is that the atmosphere is violence free and that a voter feels absolutely secure to cast his/her vote in favour of a candidate of his/her choice on his/her own volition. The voters should also feel that the election machinery is impartial and that its authority is accepted without any question.

By taking certain administrative actions against the officers involved in election related work as referred to earlier, the Commission tried to convince the public in general and the voters in particular that any lapse on the part of the election machinery would not be tolerated. This was the first requirement to generate confidence in the minds of the voters.

As the election process started with the issue of notification by the Governor, an elaborate Model Code of Conduct was brought into force and it remained in operation till the election process was over. A complete ban was imposed on transfer and posting of officers and staff who would be utilized in election related work and this ban was enforced strictly. The government could transfer such officers and staff only with the approval of the Commission. There was also complete ban on ceremonial inauguration or laying of foundation stone of any project or distribution of loans etc. by ministers or any politician. In fact, the Commission refused permission to inaugurate certain programmes by the Chief Minister as it would be in violation of the Model Code of Conduct. There was also complete ban on the ministers combining official work with political work and preferential treatment in providing accommodation in government Rest Houses to ministers and other politicians. There was also restriction on the candidates regarding use of vehicles and other means for canvassing. All these restrictions were given wide publicity by the print media.

With the enforcement of the Model Code of Conduct during election to the Panchayats, I noticed the distinction between the Commission and the various government departments getting blurred. Thus when a department required approval of the Commission for transfer and posting of its officers and staff and for execution of certain schemes, it would send the files or even address a letter directly to the Commissioner and sometimes send an office note. It seemed that the government departments were considering the Commission as one of the government departments. I immediately instructed my officers that all such files, as also any office notes endorsed to the Commission, should be returned to the department forthwith and it be conveyed that any proposal on which approval of the Commission was necessary should be endorsed in a self-contained letter addressed to the Secretary of the Commission otherwise no action would be taken on such requests. The departments of the government followed this instruction of the Commission. However, it was realized later that in the absence of any election to the Panchayats or the Urban Local Bodies many departments of the government did not have any idea about the constitutional status of the Commission leading to initial confusion. Things have, however, completely changed by now and the independent status of the Commission outside the government is accepted by everybody.

As stated earlier, there was unprecedented enthusiasm among the rural people, specially women. Women candidates moved in groups for canvassing. Some district election officers had told me that in many cases four different women candidates for four different posts had canvassed together seeking womens votes. It was widely believed that such joint appeals by women candidates got impressive response from women. Women participation in election made a qualitative change in the rural areas as nobody could dare to do anything unbecoming to intimidate or insult women. Such free movement of women candidates in large numbers gradually inspired confidence among people that election would be peaceful and violence-free.

Though elections to the Panchayats and the municipalities were on non-party basis, it would be unrealistic to think that political parties would not take interest in the election. Thus by putting restrictions on transfer and posting of officers and enforcing Model Code of Conduct any interference by the party in power was curtailed. However, there was subtle attempt by certain ministers of the State government to circumvent the restrictions imposed by the Commission by undertaking private visits to their constituencies to influence election results. When this was brought to the notice of the Commission specific action was taken in individual cases besides enforcing the general restrictions. In one case it was reported to the Commission that a senior cabinet minister had made an unscheduled visit to certain areas and he was found intimidating the officers in favour of certain candidates of his choice. A telephonic message was conveyed to the minister through his office that he should return to Patna immediately otherwise the matter would be reported to the Governor. The particular minister telephoned me and sought my permission to return to headquarters early next morning on the plea that by the time he got the message from the Commission it was quite late and travelling by road at that hour of the day would be unsafe for him. I declined to give any permission except telling him that the Commission would not change its mind and it was upto him to act. Early next morning around 7.00 A.M. the minister personally telephoned me to inform that he had reached the headquarters. But the morning newspapers had already given wide publicity on their front pages about this incident and by that time the message of the Commission was loud and clear. The Commission, therefore, addressed a letter to the Chief Secretary with copies to all the departmental secretaries with a request that henceforth a copy of the tour programme of the ministers should be sent in advance to the Commission for information. The result was that the ministers started sending their tour programmes through their personal staff who would wait at the Commission to get its prior approval.

I have only referred to some of the actions taken by the Commission which completely changed the atmosphere in the State and the entire election process was completed in an orderly manner.

The steps taken by the Commission, no doubt, instilled a sense of fear among the anti-social elements. Nevertheless, the anti-social elements tried to disturb the election process on the very first day through certain mischiefs which, no doubt, created some panic in the minds of the polling personnel. The first day of poll was April 11, 2001 and the happenings on this day would have impact on the subsequent days. I would specially mention certain incidents on the first day of poll. The voters were out in large numbers and the electronic media flashed throughout the day long queues of male and female voters colourfully attired. Such impressive turn-out of voters completely demoralized and frustrated the potential trouble makers. With such large number of women voters with their children, these anti-social elements could not dare to create any violence near the polling stations as it would have harmed the women and the children, many of whom could be the relatives or acquaintances of the trouble makers. The Commission had also appealed through newspaper advertisements that the women candidates and voters would be somebody's mother, aunt, daughter, daughter-in-law etc. and, therefore, anybody contemplating violence should also think about the consequences of such violence on the women and children.

Though the anti-social elements did not succeed in

creating much disturbance near the polling stations, they devised a very novel way of showing their utter frustration. Some of these miscreants entered the polling stations as voters with some coloured liquids which they poured either in the ballot boxes containing polled ballot papers or on the ballot papers kept on the Presiding Officer's table and ran away before the security personnel could apprehend them. Since the polling personnel were tense in anticipation of violence, the Presiding Officers in some of the polling stations got so panicky and they packed up and left the polling stations much before the completion time of polling. In fact, some of the polling parties left the polling stations before 1.00 P.M. This was highlighted by the local print media the next morning.

Polling for the second phase was to take place on April 15, 2001. Thus when the Commission came to know through newspapers next day about the antics of the anti-social elements pouring coloured liquid into the ballot boxes, prompt action was taken and detailed guidelines were issued to the Returning Officers to tackle such situations. The Commission made it clear that no election would be cancelled simply because coloured liquids were poured into ballot boxes and that a final decision on whether such soiled and damaged ballot papers would be counted or not would be taken at the time of counting. In other words, if a ballot paper was damaged beyond recognition only then such a ballot paper would be rejected. Even in such cases repoll would take place only if the number of rejected ballot papers on account of the damage would affect the final result of the election. This was given wide publicity by the print media with the result that the anti-social elements failed to affect the morale of the polling personnel. This, however, did not prevent the miscreants from coming up with fresh ingenuity. A miscreant would go inside the polling station as a voter carrying sand in his shirt pockets and suddenly would throw it in the eyes of the Presiding Officer and in the confusion run away with the polled ballot boxes and throw these in the nearby pond. However, the polling personnel could not be demoralized through such antics and in many cases the miscreants were chased away and the ballot boxes recovered. This changed the scenario completely as every subsequent phase in the election was an improvement on the previous phase.

Thus taking all the above mentioned factors into consideration, the Commission considered the first day of poll, i.e., April 11, 2001 as a day of reckoning not only for the Commission but also for democracy at the grassroots level and the happenings on this day led to an orderly election in the subsequent phases.

The Commission is of the view that elections to the Panchayats as also to the municipalities were reasonably fair and the overall atmosphere in the State was conducive to a fair election. But was it free as well? That is to say, whether the law and order situation could instil a sense of security in voters to cast their votes freely without any intimidation either through allurement of money or intimidation through muscle power.

It is an accepted fact that the contesting candidates have to spend a lot of money in printing publicity materials and for various activities during the course of canvassing. During the past more than 50 years or so of Indian democracy, the country has witnessed several elections to the State Legislature and to Parliament and the people are now used to the contesting candidates spending a lot of money. However, not many had imagined that the contesting candidates for Panchayat elections would spend considerable amount of money. There is no legal provision to put a ceiling on the expenditure to be incurred by a candidate in Panchayat elections although such provisions exist for municipal polls. However, it was difficult to ensure compliance with the ceiling of expenditure for election to the municipalities as the amount prescribed was very low. Nevertheless, an attempt was made to evolve some norms to make the candidates at least conscious that their expenditure was being monitored. Accordingly, I fixed different rates per day per vehicle such as four wheelers, three wheelers, two wheelers with differential rates depending on owner vehicle or friend's vehicle or vehicle provided by taxi services. Rates for use of cycle rickshaw, expenses on food etc. for workers and for publicity materials like big/small hoardings and pamphlets/ hand-bills etc. were also prescribed. Though the District Election Officers in their own way tried to enforce the instructions, the Commission itself did not make any effort to physically verify the actual level of expenditure which would, no doubt, be quite high depending on the perception of individual candidates as had happened during election to Panchayats. But there was no rumour of monetary inducements being given to the voters for voting in favour of a candidate. There was no report or even speculation that candidates for election to the Panchayats were alluring the voters through money. Moreover, election to the Panchayats specially for the post of a member of a Gram Panchayat is so localized that any candidate trying to influence voters through monetary or other material inducement would be exposed immediately and such a candidate would be looked down upon by the society. Nevertheless, as believed in some circles, candidates for the post of Mukhiya of the Gram Panchayat and for the post of member of Zila Parishad had spent huge amount of money. Such expenditure was rumoured to be anything between Rs. 100,000 and Rs. 500,000 per candidate for the post of Mukhiya while that for the post of member of a Zila Parishad it might have crossed Rs. one million. As indicated earlier, there was general belief that huge monetary grants would be available to the Gram Panchayat to be spent on development activities under the supervision of the Mukhiya. Similarly the chairperson of the Zila Parishad would be a very important office in the overall planning of developmental activities. Therefore, the quantum of money that was spent during election to the Panchayats by a particular candidate would depend on his prospect of winning the post of a Mukhiya or the post of the chairperson of the Zila Parishad.

Coming to the question of influencing voters through intimidation by the anti-social and criminal elements it would be pertinent to make a distinction between the anti-social or criminal activities in the context of election, whether to the Local Bodies or to the State Legislature or Parliament. The society is always confronted with two types of anti-social elements many of whom would also be liable for action under the criminal laws. The society has its own norms to treat an anti-social person and the entire society generally follows those norms. But these social or ethical norms are different from the norms in deciding the criminal background of the contesting candidates in an election. The society takes into account both the covert and overt actions of an individual in declaring such an individual anti-social while the criminal laws take cognizance of only the overt action of the individual which is punishable by a criminal court. Thus we should not confuse between the social or ethical norms and the anti-social or criminal background of an individual under the criminal laws. This is perhaps the reason why a particular candidate who is treated by the society as anti-social with muscle power to terrorize the people in general and the voters in particular and to intimidate the voters in his favour still cannot be disqualified under the electoral laws for contesting election. Therefore, the Commission or any election machinery is severely handicapped because of the legal impediments and loopholes in eliminating candidates with criminal antecedent in any election.

We may now look at the relevant provisions under the Constitution and the three Acts passed by State Legislature, one for election to the three-tier Panchayat Institutions, the other two for the Urban Local Bodies on the question of disqualifications of a candidate which empower the Returning Officer to reject nomination filed by any person so disqualified under the law.

Article 243-F of the Constitution provides for disqualification for membership of a Panchayat which is extracted below:

243-F. Disqualification for Membership

1. A person shall be disqualified for being chosen as, and for being, a member of Panchayat—
   (*a*) if he is so disqualified by or under any law for the time being in force for the purposes of

elections to the Legislature of the State concerned:

Provided that no persons shall be disqualified on the ground that he is less than twenty-five years of age, if he has attained the age of twenty-one years;

(*b*) if he is so disqualified by or under any law made by the Legislature of the State.

2. If any question arises as to whether a member of a Panchayat has become subject to any of the disqualifications mentioned in clause (1), the question shall be referred for the decision of such authority and in such manner as the Legislature of a State may, by law, provide.

In pursuance of the provisions under clause (1) (b) of the above Article the Bihar Panchayat Raj Act, 1993 (Act) has been enacted by the State Legislature. Sub-sections (1) and (2) of section 139 of the Act deal with the question of disqualification and the same are extracted below:—

Section 139

1. Notwithstanding anything contained in this Act, a person shall be disqualified for election or after election for holding the post as Mukhiya, member of the Gram Panchayat, Sarpanch, Panch of the Gram Katchahri, member of the Panchayat Samiti and member of Zila Parishad, if such person—

   (*a*) is not citizen of India;

   (*b*) is so disqualified by or under any law for the time being in force for the purposes of elections to the Legislature of the State:

   Provided that no person shall be disqualified on the ground that he is less than twenty-five years of age, if he has attained the age of twenty-one years;

   (*c*) is in the service of Central or State government or any local authority;

(*d*) is in service of any such institution receiving aids from Central or State government or any local authority;

(*e*) has been adjudged by a competent court to be of unsound mind;

(*f*) has been dismissed from the service of Central or State government or any local authority for misconduct and has been declared to be disqualified for employment in the public service;

(*g*) has been sentenced by a criminal court whether within or without India to imprisonment for an offence, other than a political offence, for a term exceeding six months or has been ordered to furnish security for good behaviour under section 109 or section 110 of the Code of Criminal Procedure, 1973 (Act 2, 1974) and such sentence or order not having subsequently been reversed.

(*h*) has under any law for the time being in force become ineligible to be a member of any local authority;

(*i*) holds any salaried office or office of profit under the Panchayat;

(*j*) has been found guilty of corrupt practices: Provided that on being found guilty of corrupt practices, the disqualification shall cease after six years of general election.

2. If any question arises as to whether a member of a Panchayat at any level has become subject to any of the disqualifications mentioned in sub-section (1), the question shall be referred for the decision of such authority and in such manner as the Government may by law provide.

Likewise Article 243-V of the Constitution deals with the question of disqualification for election as a member of a municipality. The Article is extracted below:

243-V. Disqualifications for Membership

1. A person shall be disqualified for being chosen as, and for being, a member of a municipality—

   (*a*) if he is so disqualified by or under any law for the time being in force for the purposes of elections to the Legislature of the State concerned:
   Provided that no person shall be disqualified on the ground that he is less than twenty-five years of age, if he has attained the age of twenty-one years;

   (*b*) if he is so disqualified by or under any law made by the Legislature of the State.

2. If any question arises as to whether a member of a municipality has become subject to any of the disqualifications mentioned in clause (1), the question shall be referred for the decision of such authority and in such manner as the Legislature of a State may, by law, provide.

In pursuance of the clause (1) (b) of the Article stated above, the Bihar Municipal Act, 1922 (Bihar Act) and the Patna Municipal Corporation Act, 1951 (Patna Act) were enacted by the State Legislature. While the Bihar Act applies to all the municipalities, i.e., Nagar Panchayat and Nagar Parishad, the Patna Act applies to the five Municipal Corporations in the State. The question of disqualifications has to be decided under section 14 of the Patna Act for the Municipal Corporation and section 17 of the Bihar Act for the other two categories of municipalities, i.e., Nagar Panchayat and Nagar Parishad. Both the sections have identical provisions on disqualifications.

Section 14 of the Patna Municipal Corporation Act is extracted below—

Section 14. Disqualifications

1. Notwithstanding anything contained in this Act, a person shall be disqualified for election or after

election for holding the post as member of the Municipal Corporation if such person—

(*a*) is not a citizen of India;

(*b*) is so disqualified by or under any law, for the time being in force, for the purpose of elections to the Legislature of the State:
Provided that no person shall be disqualified on the ground that he is less than twenty-five years of age, if he has attained the age of twenty-one years;

(*c*) is in the service of Central or State government or any local Authority;

(*d*) is in service of any such institution receiving aids from Central or State government or any local authority;

(*e*) has been adjudged by a competent court to be of unsound mind;

(*f*) has been dismissed from the service of Central or State government or any local authority for misconduct and has been declared to be disqualified for employment in the public service;

(*g*) has been sentenced by a criminal court, whether within or without India, to imprisonment for an offence, other than a political offence, for a term exceeding six months or has been ordered to furnish security for keeping good behaviour under section 109 or section 110 of the Code of Criminal Procedure, 1973 (Act 2, 1974) and such sentence or order not having subsequently been reversed;

(*h*) has under any law for the time being in force become ineligible to be a member of any local authority;

(*i*) holds any salaried office or office of profit under the Municipal Corporation;

(*j*) has been found guilty of corrupt practices:

Provided that on being found guilty of corrupt practices, the disqualification shall cease after six years of general election;

(*k*) if he has not paid all taxes due by him to the Municipal Corporation at the end of the financial year immediately preceding that in which the election is held.

2. If any question arises as to whether a member of a Municipal Corporation has become subject to any of the disqualification mentioned in sub-section (1), the question shall be decided by such authority and in such manner as may be prescribed.

Section 17 of the Bihar Municipal Act is extracted below:

Section 17. Disqualifications

1. Notwithstanding anything contained in this Act, a person shall be disqualified for election or after election for holding the post as member of the municipality if such person—

    (*a*) is not a citizen of India;

    (*b*) is so disqualified by or under any law, for the time being in force, for the purpose of elections to the Legislature of the State:
    Provided that no person shall be disqualified on the ground that he is less than twenty-five years of age, if he has attained the age of twenty-one years;

    (*c*) is in the service of Central or State government or any local Authority;

    (*d*) is in service of any such institution receiving aids from Central or State government or any local authority;

    (*e*) has been adjudged by a competent court to be of unsound mind;

    (*f*) has been dismissed from the service of Central

or State government or any local authority for misconduct and has been declared to be disqualified for employment in the public service;

(*g*) has been sentenced by a criminal court, whether within or without India, to imprisonment for an offence, other than a political offence, for a term exceeding six months or has been ordered to furnish security for keeping good behaviour under section 109 or section 110 of the Code of Criminal Procedure 1973 (Act 2, 1974) and such sentence or order not having subsequently been reversed;

(*h*) has under any law for the time being in force become ineligible to be a member of any local authority;

(*i*) holds any salaried office or office of profit under the municipality;

(*j*) has been found guilty of corrupt practices: Provided that on being found guilty of corrupt practices, the disqualification shall cease after six years of general election;

(*k*) if he has not paid all taxes due by him to the municipality at the end of the financial year immediately preceding that in which the election is held.

2. If any question arises as to whether a member of a municipality has become subject to any of the disqualification mentioned in sub-section (1), the question shall be decided by such authority and in such manner as may be prescribed.

It will be seen that clause (*g*) of sub-section (1) of section 139 of the Act (Panchayat) and clause (*g*) of sub-section (1) of both the sections under the two Acts applicable for the Municipalities and Municipal Corporations contain identical provisions regarding criminal background of a contesting candidate and, in the context of the election, the Commission is concerned only with this particular clause in rejecting the nomination filed by a person with criminal background. The provisions make it very clear that a person shall be disqualified for election only if he has been sentenced for an offence, other than a political offence, for a term exceeding six months or has been ordered to furnish security for good behaviour under section 109 or section 110 of the Code of Criminal Procedure (Cr.P.C.) and that such sentence or order has not been quashed subsequently. Thus a person who suffers from the above disqualification can be prevented from contesting an election. Besides the above disqualification, there are other disqualifications under all the three Acts. However, the question of criminal background of a candidate is to be decided only under the specific clause (g) as explained above.

It will, therefore, be clear that there are two ingredients of disqualification under clause (g), i.e., conviction by a criminal court. One is that the period of imprisonment awarded by a competent criminal court shall exceed six months. In other words, if the period of imprisonment is less than six months the person is not covered under the said disqualification. Likewise, there has to be a specific order by the competent authority under section 109 or section 110 of the Cr.P.C. for keeping good behaviour. The other ingredient is that the award of sentence or the order for good behaviour has not been set aside by a competent court of law/authority. This question had been finally settled by the Supreme Court in Writ Petitions (C) No. 242/2001 with others decided on September 21, 2001 in B.R. Kapur *Vs.* State of Tamil Nadu and another reproduced in (2001) 7 Supreme Court Cases 231 *vide* paras 40 and 44 of the above noted judgement. The Apex Court made it absolutely clear that the order of conviction and sentence shall remain operative and consequently the disqualification shall also continue until the order of conviction and sentence are set aside in appeal. The same logic will follow in respect of any order for keeping good behaviour. The Apex Court also made it clear that grant of bail or pendency of an appeal cannot be a ground for excluding a convicted person from the ambit of disqualification under the relevant Act.

No doubt, there is a legal provision under sub-section (1) of section 139 of the Act to prevent persons with the above disqualification from contesting election to the Panchayat. But the question is how would the Returning Officer know if a particular person suffers from the above disqualification while receiving his nomination. It becomes all the more difficult if nobody at the time of scrutiny of nomination brings it to the notice of the Returning Officer that a particular person has the above disqualification. There could be various reasons as people in general might not be aware that a particular candidate was convicted by a criminal court and imprisoned for more than six months or people might be afraid of subsequent revengeful act if anybody reports to the Returning Officer against him. Moreover, the people in general might not also be aware of the legal provisions regarding disqualifications as the election to the Panchayats was being held after 23 years under a new Act. The Commission, therefore, incorporated it in the instructions issued by it on filing and receiving nomination. It was made mandatory that all nominations be accompanied by an affidavit, duly sworn in before a Magistrate or a Notary Public in a format prescribed by the Commission. The affidavit required the candidate to make a deposition that he was fully conversant with the provisions of disqualifications under section 139 of the Act with a further declaration that he was not ineligible for election or after election for holding the post under the Act. A specimen of the affidavit is in Appendix-C. In the absence of any legal basis there was no other practical methodology which could be adopted by the Returning Officer to be reasonably sure that a person with criminal background would not contest election because a person filing false affidavit could be subsequently prosecuted under the relevant provisions of the Indian Penal Code.

Despite all the precautions taken by the Commission it was not possible to altogether prevent convicted persons from contesting election and getting elected. The local print media widely reported that a large number of convicted persons were elected to the various posts of the Panchayats. This matter was brought to the notice of the Patna High Court in one on-going Public Interest Litigation (PIL) during the course of hearing. Although there was a provision in the Rules to decide the question of disqualification by the Munsiff Magistrate, the State government amended the relevant rule 122 of the Bihar Panchayat Election Rules, 1995 with effect from February 28, 2002 vesting the power in the State Election Commission. The amended rule 122 is extracted below:

> **Rule 122:** Under provisions of section 139(2) of the Bihar Panchayati Raj Act, 1993, the State Election Commission shall be the competent authority to decide whether a member of a panchayat at any level has become subject to any of the disqualifications mentioned in section 139 (1) of the Act. The matter of disqualification may be brought to the notice of the State Election Commission in the form of a complaint, application or information by any person or authority. The State Election Commission may also take *suo motu* congnizance of such matters and decide such matters expeditiously after allowing sufficient opportunity to the affected parties of being heard.

The Commission had been deciding such question since July, 2002 and till March 15, 2003 the Commission disposed of 100 cases out of the total 121 cases filed before it. The Commission had so far disqualified 55 convicted persons from the elected posts and all these posts had been declared as vacant. Of these 55 disqualified persons, 42 were Mukhiyas of the Gram Panchayats, three were members of the Zila Parishads, six were members of the Panchayat Samitis and four were members of the Gram Panchayats. Majority of such disqualified elected members are convicted persons. The Commission, however, exonerated 45 elected persons against whom cases were filed. This was also widely publicized by the print media with the result that the people are now coming forward on their own with petitions against such convicted or otherwise disqualified persons who managed to get elected to various posts in the Panchayats. Four of such decisions of the Commission are in Appendices F, G, H and I. The above decisions would give an idea about the political awareness of the elected representatives who had taken recourse to all conceivable interpretations of the various legal provisions so as to stick to the posts they were elected to. Accordingly, I decided to put four such decisions taken by me as the State Election Commissioner in the Appendices.

That the convicted persons have a great stake in the proceedings before the Commission is proved by the fact that most of them engaged very senior advocates during hearing which continued for several days and, therefore, might have spent a lot of money on litigation. Nevertheless, if we look at the figure of 55 disqualified persons on account of their conviction by a criminal court or other disqualifications against a total number of 1,37,273 posts in the Panchayats it would not project an alarming situation and would not also look quite unusual in the context of the general criminal-politician nexus. Even with the deterrent legal provisions, people tried to take advantage of the loopholes in the law. For example, *political offence* has been excluded from the purview of disqualification without giving any definition of *political offence* in the Act or in the Rules. This prompted a convicted person to argue before the Commission that he had murdered a person due to political rivalry and, therefore, he could not be treated as disqualified under the law. In fact, he had gone to the extent of equating his act of killing with the act of killings of British people during freedom movement of the country. The Commission treated such submissions with the contempt these deserved but such pleadings only reflect the stakes the elected representatives have in election to the Panchayats.

We have seen that mandatory submission of an affidavit along with the nomination paper did not prove effective in eliminating convicted persons from the field of election to the Panchayats as many of them contested election and also got elected. The Commission, learning from its experience during Panchayat election, made it mandatory for a candidate in Municipal elections to file a declaration in Appendices D and E, prescribed by the Commission, about his criminal background and criminal cases pending against him along with his nomination. Such a declaration should be signed by him along with signatures of two witnesses with their full names and addresses during election to the municipalities which took place after a year. This measure, i.e. signature of two witnesses on the declaration was an effective check as the witnesses would sign any such declaration only after ascertaining the authenticity of the contents of the declaration. These steps taken by the Commission during election to the municipalities proved very effective as there was no report of any person with criminal background being elected as a Ward Commissioner/Ward Councillor of any municipality. This was no mean achievement considering the fact that the general crime graph in the State was a matter of concern for everybody. The Commission could not get the benefit of the order of the Supreme Court passed subsequently on May 2, 2002 regarding declaration to be furnished by a candidate for State Legislature/Parliament. The three Acts governing election to the Panchayats and municipalities referred to earlier do not have any provision regarding affidavit to be furnished by a contesting candidate. The Commission, therefore, exercised its plenary power under the Constitution by issuing instructions making it mandatory for the contesting candidates to furnish the affidavit and the declaration.

Another peculiar phenomenon that came to light after the election was that many convicted and disqualified elected members of Panchayats did not take oath as they were absconding for fear of getting arrested. These candidates had filed their nominations through their election agents and, therefore, they could not be apprehended by the police at the time of filing nomination.

There is no provision in the law for filing nomination in person only and due to shortage of time the Commission could not go into greater details on this issue. It was, therefore, made obligatory for a candidate in municipal elections to file his nomination in person before the Returning Officer and since there was enough time appropriate provisions had also been made in the relevant Rules. This proved to be a very effective step in keeping away criminals and convicted persons who were absconding for fear of getting arrested from filing nomination in the urban polls held after a year.

In spite of my best efforts I was not able to completely cleanse the electoral field during election to the Panchayats, but some concrete steps taken would go a long way in preventing persons with criminal background from contesting election to the Panchayats. In fact, the election held subsequently to the Urban Local Bodies proved my point and with the political awareness and the knowledge of the legal provisions, specially the decisions of the Commission unseating few elected members of the Panchayats that got wide publicity through the print media, would hopefully, ensure that in the 2006 polls no disqualified person is able to contest election to the Panchayats. This is proved by the fact that during the course of hearing on disqualification the Commission was surprised to see that some public spirited persons had filed petitions against certain elected members of the Panchayats who were disqualified on account of their holding a post of profit or for not being a citizen of India or other disqualifications as enumerated under sub-section (1) of section 139 of the Act.

I have briefly narrated the legal provisions and the steps taken by the Commission to check criminalization of politics in election to the rural and urban Local Bodies. I would now refer to certain important facts and it is for the readers to judge whether in the given circumstances conduct of elections to the Panchayats and the municipalities was free enabling voters to exercise their right of franchise in a conducive atmosphere.

The scale of violence in a State should be judged with reference to the general crime graph of the State and not in isolation. The local newspapers have given wide coverage to the instructions, guidelines and decisions taken by the Commission. The people in general and the voters in particular were adequately educated about the authority of the Commission. The electronic media also gave wide coverage by flashing long queues of male and female voters in various polling stations. Therefore, people could see for themselves the qualitative change in the overall atmosphere which would be conducive to holding election in an orderly manner. However, some sort of exaggerated apprehension about the likely violence during the poll as also some eye-catching headlines on the front pages of the print media, specially after the first day of poll, could have been avoided because such news at that time might mislead the unsuspecting people. Perhaps prevalent illiteracy (inability to read newspapers) proved a blessing in disguise for the simple and illiterate but not so unintelligent voters to make their own conclusion. As stated earlier, the visuals of long queues of female voters in their colourful attire shown by electronic media throughout the day on the days of poll demolished the print media reports about the so-called scale of violence.

There was no dispute on the inevitability of violence during polls but only on the scale of such violence. A public debate started on the issue with predictions by so-called well informed but self-opinionated persons on the number of casualties likely to take place. From the floor figure of more than 700 deaths in last Panchayat polls in 1978 the casualty figure for this poll was pegged at 5,000 in view of average daily crime rate of ten. Local newspapers came out with headings like *"chunao ke nam par Bihar me khoon ki Holi kheli ja rahi hai"* (in the name of election the festival of Holi in blood is being played in Bihar). Different newspapers were giving different casualty figures widely varying between 16 and 30. There was also a report that *"Bihar me rakta Ganga baha raha hai"*(Ganges of blood is flowing in Bihar). It was a great relief that other rivers like Punpun, Gandak or Kosi were spared. However, as the election process progressed such reporting became more restrained. During one of my rare press conferences (every information was being given to the press regularly by the public relation section of the Commission) I asked the reporters as to how they were collecting the casualty figures as every such death on account of violence etc. is always routinely registered in the local police station. They had no answer and subsequently a local vernacular newspaper with wide circulation started giving district-wise figures only to prove the authenticity of reports. However, things became a bit difficult for the newspapers as the number of deaths during elections did not even touch 100 which was way behind the figure of 700 of 1978. In view of the prepoll predictions of likely violence surpassing the 1978 casualties it was the base figure that saw downward revisions. First it came down to this figure of 700 which was subsequently revised downward to a figure of 500 quoting as source the debate in the State Legislature. All of a sudden a magic figure of 95 was reported as the figure of casualties during the election in 1978. This was perhaps inescapable as the earlier apprehension was that the casualty figures would surpass those of 1978 and such a prediction could materialize only if the actual figure in 2001 would be more than the figures of 1978. Since the casualty figures in election in April-May, 2001 were doubtful of touching even 100, one had to reduce the figure of casualties during 1978 to a figure below 100 so that the prediction of higher figures of casualties could not go wrong. At the end of the election one leading daily worked out a figure of casualties at 200 and this was published in a box news on the front page of the paper, perhaps as an authentic piece of documentary evidence for reference purposes during the next election.

As against the apprehended violence narrated in the preceding paragraphs one must look at certain very relevant facts before one comes to a conclusion about the scale of poll related violence that took place in Bihar during election to the Panchayats in April-May, 2001. I am stating those facts in the sequel.

The voting percentage varied between 60 and 75 and in many polling stations it crossed 95 per cent. The suspected cases of booth capturing detected during the process of counting did not confirm that rigging had taken place widely. Even newspaper reports did not highlight large scale booth capturing. In fact, the spirited protest by women voters in a polling station in Maner near Patna, which was highlighted in the newspapers the next morning with photographs of the women voters raising slogans against the high handedness of the feudal male elements trying to prevent women from casting their votes further emboldened the voters to come out in large numbers to exercise their franchise. The situation at Maner became so tense that the district administration had to rush to the area and the women refused to relent and could not be controlled till they were allowed to cast their votes. Incidents like this only proved that the voters were free to exercise their democratic rights.

As stated earlier, the women voters were out in large numbers which was flashed on the TV. At a particular polling station there was a lot of commotion in the male queue without any effect on the female queue in the same polling station. Despite threats of violence due to the commotion in the male queue the females stood patiently in their queues. This was projected by the electronic media contributing to a very healthy atmosphere during the election process.

It is a common knowledge in India specially in the rural areas that people do not allow womenfolk to go out if there is even remote apprehension of violence. Thus in spite of fears expressed by the so-called well informed people and the print media the "little man" exercised his right of franchise without any fear.

In efforts to prevent voters from stepping out by instilling fear a big article recalled the horrors of Belchi, a place very close to Patna, that took place way back in 1978 and till then was the largest ever massacre. This incident was also politically significant. These brutal killings were condemned by all the newspapers. Late Prime Minister Indira Gandhi, then out of power, utilised this opportunity and undertook the famous elephant ride to Belchi holding an umbrella over her head which was widely publicized by all the national newspapers besides the local dailies. It was then generally believed that this elephant ride returned Mrs. Gandhi to the centre-stage of Indian politics after the premature collapse of the Janata Government at the Centre. A vernacular daily with a wide circulation came out with the article in its edition on April 14, 2001 recalling the scale of brutality and highlighting the so-called fear under which the people in that area were supposedly waiting for a repeat of Belchi the next day, i.e., April 15, the day of poll. 23 years had since passed and still the newspaper did not find any other opportune moment to refer to certain happenings which every civilized society would like to forget. But much to the discomfiture of the learned scholar, who penned the article, the voters exercised their rights of franchise peacefully.

What is quite significant about the figures of casualty is that not a single person was killed anywhere near the polling station. In fact, poll related killings did not exceed 50 and the total figure of killings during the entire period would be below 100 in all. Certain unfortunate incidents took place during poll in which some precious lives of innocent people were lost and most of the casualties took place in group clashes between the supporters mostly of the candidates for the post of Mukhiya and at places far away from the polling stations. Some women and children became victims of cross firing. It will be unrealistic to think that in a State where the general crime graph is always high, the criminals would turn law-abiding overnight and completely withdraw from the field of their activities on the day of poll for the sake of ushering in grassroots democracy.

Another striking feature was that not a single personnel of the polling parties was killed or even injured. A few unfortunate incidents like the killing of a Magistrate on law and order duty in Jamui who was fired at when he attempted to stop rigging at a particular polling station did take place. The particular officer was not a regular Magistrate and perhaps this was the reason for him being a bit less tactful and cautious. The other two or three incidents were deaths of some homeguards on duty. The State Government anticipated more casualties and accordingly it had paid a premium of Rs. 40 million to the Insurance Company while the actual claim was about Rs. 4 million.

Some of the brave actions of polling personnel are worth mentioning. In some cases the Presiding Officers chased the miscreants and recovered the ballot papers and polled ballot boxes. In a north Bihar district a notorious criminal shot at a Homeguard jawan whose rifle fell on the ground. Despite being shot at the jawan picked up the rifle and killed the criminal on the spot. In another case the police on duty at a polling station chased some miscreants who were running away with the polled ballot boxes and killed them and recovered the boxes.

I have narrated briefly some of the facts which would prove beyond doubt that election to the three-tier Panchayat Institutions was orderly and reasonably free of violence. Thus the general perception that Bihar would never have grassroots democracy in operation and that too in a peaceful and orderly way has been proved wrong if we look at the overall picture of election to the three-tier Panchayat Institutions. Various factors are responsible for such an achievement.

As stated earlier, people for the first time exercised their right of franchise in Panchayat elections after 1978. At that time the minimum age for voting was 21 years which is now 18. Such voters who were born in or after 1957 exercised their right of franchise for the first time in about 44 years in any election to the Panchayats. This younger generation of voters made a qualitative change in the electoral scenes in the rural areas. The 50 years of Indian democracy has made them politically conscious and they have seen the spoils of democratic process enjoyed by their elected representatives who would make quinquennial sojourn to their constituencies at the time of election to the State Legislative Assembly or the Parliament. The younger generation is fed up with the absentee representatives who would mostly be staying at Patna and their voters would be left to themselves. Thus the decision of the government to revive the Panchayati Raj Institutions created an unprecedented enthusiasm in the rural areas and the people wanted an Institution at their doorsteps which they indeed got through the election.

Reservation of seats for the Scheduled Castes, the Scheduled Tribes and the women created a ray of hope among the disadvantaged section of the society and they came in large numbers to take part in the election. The women power once out, is out with all fury as proved by the Maner incident. Failure of the State government and the elected representatives of the people to improve the delivery system under various well conceived rural development projects has completely frustrated the rural people and they had utilized the opportunity to express their anguish through ballots and it was not surprising that most of the sitting Mukhiyas (Mukhiyas elected in the last election) who were also a party to the abject condition in the rural areas were shown the door with very few of them managing to get re-elected.

Whether an election has been free and fair should not be judged only by the number of persons killed during the process, though it is a relevant factor, but from the overall atmosphere enabling ordinary voters to feel free and confident and come out on their own to cast their votes in favour of the candidates of their choice. We may visualize a situation when incident of violence would be nil due to the terror tactics of the musclemen of the influential candidates and the voters would be terrorized to vote only in favour of a particular candidate. Obviously, such an election cannot be called free and fair, but nevertheless, violence-free. The last election to the Jammu and Kashmir State Assembly was undoubtedly a classic case of free and fair election and acclaimed as such even by the international community, not all necessarily friendly to India. Still we cannot say that the overall situation in the State, specially in the valley, was not tense. Long queues of voters, including women, in the interior and flashed by independent TV channels throughout the day proved that the voters felt free and confident to brave the atmosphere, which might not be the most ideal one in a State where killings of innocent people by the militants are facts of life, and to came out in good numbers on their own to exercise their right of franchise. How could such a miracle happen? The answer was a person by the name J.M. Lyngdoh, the Chief Election Commissioner of India, who silently, and without any show, but firmly let the political class behave. It is the impartial stand and firmness of the Election Commission that makes all the difference. I was quite amused when a very senior bureaucrat of Bihar, who is known for his cynical approach, commented that the voters in Jammu and Kashmir came out in good numbers only to see the Electronic Voting Machine (EVM) as if it (EVM) was too attractive a toy to ignore the threat posed by the militants who were still there to terrorise the people.

A look at the election scenario in Bihar, where violence is almost a way of life and where the daily figure of casualties is more than ten regardless of election, it could be concluded that elections to the Panchayats and the municipalities were reasonably free and fair. Else how could one justify the long queues of voters, women outnumbering the males in many booths, with an average voting percentage touching more than 65? Even the cases of rigging reported by the print media were very small. This belied the initial predictions widely reported by the print media that Bihar would witness a bloody and rigged poll. In Bihar, the people in rural areas were determined to demolish the iron grip of the vested interests and, therefore, they could read the actions taken by the State Election Commission and felt absolutely free and confident to come out in large numbers which baffled the political pundits.

I would not show the temerity to claim that the Commission should appropriate the entire credit for the victory of ballots over bullets. But the Commission, which was still a nascent body, had, in its limited way under the given circumstances in the State, done everything that was humanly possible to create an atmosphere for the "little man" in the rural areas to brave all provocations of apprehended violence and to exercise his right of franchise silently. The voters rarely committed any mistake, as proved during counting of votes, in marking four different ballot papers simultaneously in favour of candidates of their choice and putting the ballot papers individually folded in one ballot box.

I think everyone should salute this "little man" who has proved that *ballot is mightier than bullet.*

7

Reservation

Reservation in the Panchayats

Reservation is not an end in itself but a means to achieve certain ends. What are these ends to be achieved through reservation? Whatever be the reasons the fact is that there is a section of society, including women, which has been traditionally disadvantaged both socially, economically and educationally. The Constitution provides equal rights for every citizen but it has not improved the social, educational and economical lot of this section of the people. Even among the so-called affluent sections of society, gender discrimination continues and the women in general always suffer the most.

It was, therefore, thought that there should be provisions of reservation for such disadvantaged section of the population in sharing power at the grassroots level so that their views are given due importance in the overall development of the rural areas where majority of the people live. One should look at the issue of reservation from this angle. There could be no two opinions on the need for providing reservation for certain sections of the people in the three-tier Panchayat Institutions. Since the post of Chairperson of a Panchayat, specially the post of Chairperson of the Gram Panchayat, is the most effective office, the need for reserving certain number of posts of Chairpersons at every level of the Panchayat system is there. Accordingly, the Constitution (73rd) Amendment Act, 1992 includes mandatory provisions under Article 243-D. Article 243-D is extracted below:

243-D. Reservation of Seats

1. Seats shall be reserved for—

   (*a*) the Scheduled Castes;
   (*b*) the Scheduled Tribes,

   in every Panchayat and the number of seats so reserved shall bear, as nearly as may be, the same proportion to the total number of seats to be filled by direct election in that Panchayat as the population of the Scheduled Castes in that Panchayat area or of the Scheduled Tribes in that Panchayat area bears to the total population of that area and such seats may be allotted by rotation to different constituency in a Panchayat.
2. Not less than one-third of the total number of seats reserved under clause (1) shall be reserved for women belonging to the Scheduled Castes or, as the case may be, the Scheduled Tribes.
3. Not less than one-third (including the number of seats reserved for women belonging to the Scheduled Castes and the Scheduled Tribes) of the total number of seats to be filled by direct election in every Panchayat shall be reserved for women and such seats may be allotted by rotation to different constituencies in a Panchayat.
4. The offices of the Chairpersons in the Panchayats at the village or any other level shall be reserved for the Scheduled Castes, the Scheduled Tribes and women in such manner as the Legislature of a State may, by law, provide:
   Provided that the number of offices of Chairpersons reserved for the Scheduled Castes and the Scheduled Tribes in the Panchayats at each level in any State shall bear, as nearly as may be, the same proportion to the total number of such offices in Panchayats at each level as the population of the Scheduled Castes in the State or of the Scheduled Tribes in the State bears to the total population of the State:

Provided further that not less than one-third of the total number of offices of Chairpersons in the Panchayats at each level shall be reserved for women: Provided also that the number of offices reserved under this clause shall be allotted by rotation to different Panchayats at each level.

5. The reservation of seats under clauses (1) and (2) and the reservation of office of Chairpersons (other than the reservation for women) under clause (4) shall cease to have effect on the expiration of the period specified in Article 334.
6. Nothing in this Part shall prevent the Legislature of a State from making any provision for reservation of seats in any Panchayat or offices of Chairpersons in the Panchayats at any level in favour of backward class of citizens.

Thus the Constitution provides for mandatory reservation of seats and of the offices of the Chairpersons in the Panchayats at the village or any other level for the Scheduled Castes, the Scheduled Tribes and Women. The Constitution also provides for calculating the number of seats as also number of offices of Chairpersons to be reserved for above categories of persons and hence there is no scope for any deviation from the mandatory provisions of the Constitution.

As stated in the beginning, reservation is not an end in itself but only a means to achieve certain end which is only the social, economic and educational upliftment of certain sections of the population. In other words, once the end is achieved there will be no need to continue the system of reservation and accordingly it has also bean provided in Article 334 of the Constitution that the reservation in favour of the Scheduled Castes and the Scheduled Tribes shall become inoperative from a particular time. Thus it was presumed that a person belonging to the Scheduled Castes and the Scheduled Tribes would not need any special privilege through reservation after a certain time. However, the same was not the case for women as the law makers thought that reservation for women should be in perpetuity and hence it would continue as a permanent feature of the Constitution. This means that the women power would remain an integral part in the all round development of the country.

Everyone of us knows that the instrument of reservation has been used in the industrial activities of the country also. Thus we have reservation in favour of small scale industries so that such industries can compete with big industries. If we do not grudge reservation in favour of small-scale industries why should we not appreciate the need for reservation in favour of certain disadvantaged sections of the population.

In terms of the provision of Article 243-D, the State Legislature enacted the Bihar Panchayat Raj Act, 1993 providing for reservation of seats and reservation of Chairpersons in the three-tier Panchayat Institutions. Accordingly, provisions were made in sections 13, 36 and 63 for reservation of seats and in sections 15, 38 and 65 for reservation of Chairpersons in the Gram Panchayat, Panchayat Samiti and Zila Parishad respectively. The above sections are extracted below:

13. Reservation of Seats

1. In every Gram Panchayat seats shall be reserved for—

   (*a*) Scheduled Castes;
   (*b*) Scheduled Tribes; and
   (*c*) Backward Classes; and

   the number of seats so reserved shall bear as nearly as may be, the same proportion to the total number of seats to be filled up by direct election in that Panchayat as the population of the Scheduled Castes/ Scheduled Tribes/or of the Backward Classes bears to the total population of that area and such seats shall be allotted by rotation to different constituencies in a Gram Panchayat in such manner as may be prescribed by the State Election Commission.

2 Not less than one-third of the total number of seats reserved under section (1) shall be reserved for women

belonging to the scheduled castes, the scheduled tribes or the backward classes as the case may be.

3. Not less than one-third (including the number of seats reserved for women belonging to the Scheduled Castes, Scheduled Tribes and the Backward Classes) of the total number of the seats to be filled by direct election in every Gram Panchayat shall be reserved for women and such seats may be allotted by rotation to different constituencies in a Gram Panchayat in such manner as may be prescribed.

36. Reservation of Seats

1. In every Panchayat Samiti seats shall be reserved for—

    (*a*) Scheduled Castes;
    (*b*) Scheduled Tribes; and
    (*c*) Backward Classes;

    and the number of seats so reserved shall bear as far as may be, the same proportion to the total number of seats to be filled by direct election in that Panchayat Samiti as the population of the Scheduled Castes/Scheduled Tribes or of the Backward Classes in that Panchayat Samiti area bear to the total population of that area and such seats shall be allotted by rotation to different constituencies in a Panchayat Samiti in such manner, as may be prescribed by the State Election Commission.
2. Not less than one-third of the total number of seats reserved under sub-section (1) shall be reserved for women belonging to the Scheduled Castes, the Scheduled Tribes or the Backward classes, as the case may be.
3. Not less than one-third (including the number of seats reserved for women belonging to the Scheduled Castes, the Scheduled Tribes and Backward Classes) of the total number of seats to be filled by direct

election in every Panchayat Samiti shall be reserved for women and such seats may be allotted by rotation to different constituencies in a Panchayat Samiti in such manner as may be prescribed.

63. *Reservation*

1. In every Zila Parishad seats shall be reserved for:-

   (*a*) Scheduled Castes;
   (*b*) Scheduled Tribes; and
   (*c*) Backward Classes;

   and the number of seats so reserved shall bear, as nearly as may be, the same proportion to the total number of seats to be filled by direct election in that Zila Parishad, as the population of the Scheduled Castes/Scheduled Tribes or of the Backward Classes in that Zila Parishad area bears to the total population of the area and such seats shall be allotted by rotation to different constituencies in a Zila Parishad in such manner as may be prescribed.
2. Not less than one-third of the total number of seats reserved under-section (1) shall be reserved for women belonging to the Scheduled Castes or Scheduled Tribes or the Backward Classes, as the case may be.
3. Not less than one-third (including the number of seats reserved for women belonging to the Scheduled Castes and the Scheduled Tribes and the Backward Classes) of the total number of seats to be filled by direct election in every Zila Parishad shall be reserved for women and such seats may be allotted by rotation to different constituencies in a Zila Parishad in such manner as may be prescribed.

15. *(7) Reservation of Seats—*

(*i*) For the post of *Mukhiya* seats shall be reserved as follows:

(*a*) Scheduled Castes;
(*b*) Scheduled Tribes; and
(*c*) Backward Classes;

In every Panchayat Samiti, seats shall be reserved for Scheduled Castes/Scheduled Tribes/Backward Classes for the posts of Mukhiya and the number of seats so reserved shall bear as nearly as possible the same proportion to the total number of seats of Mukhiya of the said Panchayat Samiti as the population of the Scheduled Castes/Scheduled Tribes/Backward Classes bears to the proportion of the total population of that area and such seats shall be allotted by rotation to different constituencies for Mukhiya of the Panchayat Samiti by the State Election Commission in the prescribed manner.

(*ii*) Not less than one-third of the total number of seats so reserved under Sub-section (i) shall be reserved for women belonging to Scheduled Castes/ Scheduled Tribes and Backward Classes as the case may be.

(*iii*) Not less than one-third (including the number of seats reserved for women belonging to Scheduled Castes/ Scheduled Tribes and Backward Classes) of the total number of seats of Mukhyia under each Panchayat Samiti shall be reserved for women and such seats shall be allotted by rotation to different Gram Panchayat of the Panchayat Samiti in such manner as may be prescribed.

38. (2) There shall be reservation for the post of Pramukh in the following manner:

(*a*) such number of offices of Pramukh of Panchayat Samities in the district shall be reserved for persons belonging to the Scheduled Castes, Scheduled Tribes and Backward Classes bearing as nearly as may be the same proportion to the total number of offices in the district, as the population of the Scheduled Castes,

Scheduled Tribes and Backward Classes in the district bears to the total population of that district;

(*b*) Not less than one-third of the total number of the offices of Pramukh of the Panchayat Samiti shall be reserved for women but not less than one-third of the total number of seats in each category be reserved for the women belonging to Scheduled Caste/ Scheduled Tribe and Backward Classes, as the case may be:

Provided that the offices reserved under this sub-clause shall be allotted by rotation to different Panchayat Samities.

Explanation—For the removal of doubts it is hereby declared that the principle of rotation for the purposes of reservation of offices under this sub-section shall commence from the first election to be held after the commencement of this Act.

65. (2) There shall be reservation for the post of Adhyaksha in the following manner:

(*a*) Such number of offices of Adhyaksha of Zila Parishads in the State shall be reserved for persons belonging to the Scheduled Castes, Scheduled Tribes and Backward Classes bearing as nearly as may be the same proportion to the total number of offices in the State, as the population of the Scheduled Castes/ Scheduled Tribes or the Backward Classes in the State bears to the total population of the State;

(*b*) Not less than one-third of the total number of the offices of Adhyaksha in the State shall be reserved for women but not less than one-third of such offices, in each category be reserved for the women belonging to Scheduled Caste/Scheduled Tribe and other Backward classes, as the case may be:

Provided that the offices reserved under this section shall be allotted by rotation to different Zila Parishads.

> *Explanation*—For the removal of doubts it is hereby declared that the principle of rotation for the purposes of reservation of offices under this sub-section shall commence from the first election to be held after the commencement of this Act.

We have seen that the State Government had earlier decided to conduct election to the Panchayats in the first half of 1996. However, the election was deferred following the order of the Patna High Court dated March 19, 1996 in CWJC No. 3351 of 1994 with 11 other CWJCs. By the above order the High Court quashed certain provisions of the Act regarding reservation for the posts of Chairpersons for the Scheduled Castes, the Scheduled Tribes and women and Backward Class of citizens while upholding the provisions for reservation of seats only in favour of the Scheduled Castes, the Scheduled Tribes and women but not for Backward Class of citizens. According to the judgement of the High Court the offices of Chairpersons cannot be reserved as each of these posts is to be treated as single post. That the concept of single post is totally alien to the provisions of the Constitution will be clear from the use of the word "Chairpersons" in the plural and taking into account all such posts in the whole State in clause (4) of Article 243-D quoted earlier. I have dealt with this question in greater detail at a later stage. The High Court quashed Schedule-I of the Act with a direction to revise the list of Backward Class of citizens as shown in Schedule-I of the Act. The reason for such direction was that there were certain Backward Castes in the list which did not require any reservation as these castes were considered by the High Court as otherwise not so Backward as to justify reservation for them.

The State government filed a Special Leave Petition *vide* SLP (Civil) No. 9724-9728 of 1996 and 9819-25 of 1996 against the order of the Patna High Court referred to above before the Supreme Court. The Supreme Court passed an interim order on July 22, 1997 with the observation that the matter should be decided by a Constitution Bench. In view of the above interim order the State government came to the conclusion that election to the Panchayats has been stayed by the Apex Court and accordingly the proposal to hold election to the Panchayats earlier could not materialize. After a gap of three years the matter came up before the Apex Court on certain Interlocutory Applications (IAs) filed by the Union of India and by the State of Bihar on which the Supreme Court passed the following interim order on August 29, 2000:

> These interlocutory applications have been filed, some by the Union of India and some by the State of Bihar, praying for early hearing of the pending appeals, and for clarification of the order dated July 22, 1997. The State of Bihar, in addition, has prayed for stay of the judgement of the Patna High Court dated March 19, 1996 passed in CWJC No 3351/1994. By the said judgement, certain provisions of the Bihar Rajya Panchayat Act, 1993 have been struck down, and the legality of that judgement is the subject matter of challenge in these appeals. Though, we agree that in view of the constitutional amendment, elections to different Panchayats should be held in accordance with this constitutional scheme, but for the present situation in the State of Bihar, responsibility is that of the Bihar Government. Taking that into consideration, the Court passed an order directing the officers of the government to remain incharge of different Panchayats. There has been some observation in the said order which has made it necessary for the Union of India to file the application for clarification inasmuch as it was thought that by the said order the elections to the Panchayat have been stayed by this Court. Having heard the learned counsel for the parties, we make it clear that there is no bar for holding elections to different Panchayats in accordance with law, as it stands today, which will be subject to the final decision in the pending appeals. So far as the prayer for early hearing of the appeals are concerned, we give liberty to the parties to mention before Honble the Chief Justice of India for early hearing as we agree with the counsel for the parties that the matter should be heard early.

After the above order of the Apex Court the State government got into action and decided to hold election to the Panchayats without reservation for the posts of Chairpersons on the ground that such a post is single in nature and, therefore, reservation for such post would amount to 100 per cent reservation which is not permissible under the law. The State government informed the Commission accordingly. While considering the request of the State government the Commission came to the conclusion that as per the interim order dated August 29, 2000 passed by the Supreme Court and quoted above reservation for the posts of Chairpersons of Panchayats is mandatory as the Supreme Court has directed that election can be held in accordance with law as it stands today and, therefore, the mandatory provisions of the Constitution for reservation for the offices of Chairpersons which are also the law as it stands today should be followed and reservation should be enforced for the posts of Chairpersons also. Accordingly, the Commission filed an Interlocutory Application (IA) before the Supreme Court *vide* IA No. 99-103/2000. The Commission has deliberated in great detail on the matter before filing the IA and it had come to the conclusion that there were strong reasons for filing the IA before the Apex Court for the clarification of the expression "law as it stands today". My reasonings for filing the IA are as follows:

The Need for Filing the Application for Clarification/Modification of the Order Dated August 29, 2000 of the Supreme Court

(*i*) The order dated August 29, 2000 was passed on the application filed by the Union of India and the State of Bihar for early hearing of the pending appeals and for clarification of the order dated July 22, 1997. The only prayer made by the State of Bihar in its application was for stay of the operation of the judgement of the Patna High Court dated March 19, 1996. It is clear that the State of Bihar did not make any specific prayer for implementing the mandatory provision of Article 243 D (4) of the Constitution regarding reservation to the offices of Chairpersons (Mukhiya, Pramukh and Adhyaksha) in the three-tier Panchayat Institutions. The reference to Articles 243D(1) and (4) in para 10 of the application of the State of Bihar is only for the purpose of upholding the manner (procedure) for effecting reservation to the offices of Chairpersons as laid down in Section 15(7) (for Mukhiya), Section 38 (2) (for Pramukh) and Section 65 (2) (for Adhyaksha) of the Bihar Panchayat Raj Act, 1993. A perusal of the provisions of the above Sections of the Act would reveal that the same relate to reservation for the post of Chairpersons not only for SC, ST and women, but also for Backward Classes. Truly speaking, the case of Backward Classes should not be clubbed with the cases of SC, ST and women as while the Constitutional provisions for reservation to the offices of Chairpersons under Article 243D(4) are specific and mandatory for SC, ST and women, the same for Backward Classes is a corollary of the enabling provision in Article 243D(6). Thus while the provisions for reservation for SC, ST and women to the offices of Chairpersons are mandatory and are integral part of the Constitution, the same for Backward Classes does not have mandatory status and therefore, any such provisions for Backward Classes provided for in the State Act must stand the test of Constitutional validity. It is, therefore, clear that the State of Bihar in its application to the Supreme Court, which was decided on August 29, 2000, did not ask for any clarification or direction regarding implementation of the mandate of article 243D(4) for reserving the offices of Chairpersons for SC, ST and women and consequently the expression "law as it stands today" used by the Supreme Court in its order dated August 29, 2000 should necessarily refer to the Constitutional provision of Article 243D(4) regarding reservation to the offices of Chairpersons for SC, ST and Women, which has been declared as a valid piece of legislation by the Patna High Court and the expression "law as it stands today" would definitely exclude the manner prescribed in the State Act regarding reservation for the Backward Classes consequent upon the enabling (not mandatory) provisions of Article 243D(6). Therefore, the State Election Commission genuinely felt that the Apex Court might give clarification/direction about the "law as it stands today" *vis-à-vis* the mandatory provision of the Constitution regarding reservation to the offices of Chairpersons for SC, ST and Women as enshrined in Article 243D(4) of the Constitution.

(*ii*) The need for the clarification has arisen on account of two circulars (No. 3817 dated October 31, 2000 and 3928 dated November 16, 2000) issued by the Department of Rural Development, government of Bihar on the subject. The relevant decision of the State government in para (v) of the circulars is extracted below:

> "There shall be no reservation of any sort for the post of Mukhiya (Chairperson in Gram Panchayat), Pramukh (Chairperson for the Panchayat Samiti) and Adyaksha (Chairperson for Zila Parishad), each of which being single post."

Since the expression "Chairpersons" in the Panchayat at village level or at any other level used in Article 243D(4) of the Constitution are in the plural and the provisions of the Article refer to the total number of each of such offices throughout the State, which is clearly more than one, the decision of the State government that there shall be no reservation of any sort for the posts of Mukhiya, Pramukh and Adhyaksha is contrary to the mandatory provisions of Article 243D(4). Hence, the State Election Commission felt the need for clarity on the subject.

(*iii*) The above decision of the State government is purported to have been taken in the light of the decision of the Patna High Court dated March 19, 1996, which is the subject matter in the appeals pending before the Supreme Court. The decision of the Government of Bihar, based on advice given by the Competent Authority, regarding the meaning of the expression "law as it stands today" is that there shall be no reservation for the post of Chairpersons in the Panchayat at any level as per the order of the Patna High Court dated March 19, 1996 to the effect that as there is only one post of Chairperson in a Panchayat, any reservation for such a single post shall amount to 100 per cent reservation which is not permissible. This will mean that the specific constitutional mandate for reservation for the post of Chairpersons in the Panchayat at every level in favour of the Scheduled Castes, the Scheduled Tribes and women as enshrined in Article 243D(4) of the Constitution cannot be implemented in the Panchayat election in Bihar. It is pertinent to mention that the Patna High Court has held the above mandate for reservation for the post of Chairpersons as constitutional, therefore, the above decision of the State government, which is against the mandatory provision of the Constitution, has created confusion in the mind of the State Election Commission and hence a clarification of the expression "law as it stands today" used by the Supreme Court in its order dated August 29, 2000 is essential. The State Election Commission is of the view that the expression "law as it stands today" means and includes the constitutional provisions in Article 243D(4) of the Constitution regarding reservation to the offices of the Chairpersons in the Panchayat for S.C., S.T. and women.

(*iv*) The Patna High Court in its order dated March 19, 1996 has held that the provision of Article 243D(4) of the Constitution of India are *intra vires* of the Constitution and the same is a valid piece of legislation. This is also the legal opinion of the State government. Therefore, the provisions of Article 243D(4) which mandate that the offices of the Chairpersons of the Panchayats at the village or any other level shall be reserved for SC, ST and women are a valid piece of legislation. If this provision of the Constitution is a valid piece of legislation according to the order of Patna High Court dated March 19, 1996 and also according to the legal opinion of the State Government, it would mean that the piece of legislation, being a part of the Constitution, is also the "law" of the land as it stands today.

(*v*) Even though the legal opinion of the State government is that Article 243D(4) regarding reservation for the posts of Mukhiyas, Pramukhs and Adhyakshas is a valid law, nevertheless it has come to the conclusion that there cannot be reservation to the posts of Mukhiya, Pramukh and Adhyaksha because each of all these posts are single in nature, therefore, reservation against such a single post would amount to 100 per cent reservation, which is not permissible under the law. This "non-application of reservation" in a single post is not in dispute or a matter of contention before the Commission. But what is not clear is about the "non-applicability of reservation" against the posts of Mukhiyas, Pramukhs and Adhyakshas as enshrined in Article 243D(4) of the Constitution, which has been accepted as a valid piece of legislation. Article 243D(4) uses the expression *Chairpersons* in the *plural* and not in the *singular* form. Therefore, this expression refers to more than one offices of Chairperson. The provisos to Article 243D(4) also use the expressions "Chairpersons" in the plural form which clearly refer to the total number of each of such posts in the whole State. Therefore, the order of the Patna High Court will apply to a post if it is only a single post and not to such posts which are more than one in number. If the legal opinion of the State government is taken to its logical corollary it can also be argued that the post of a Member in a Constituency (ward) under the jurisdiction of a Gram Panchayat or a Panchayat Samiti or a Zila Parishad is also a single post in the ward concerned and, therefore, any reservation against such a post will also amount to 100 per cent reservation. If in the case of members, one takes the plea that such number of members under the jurisdiction of any Panchayat is more than one and, therefore, reservation against such total number of members would not amount to 100 per cent reservation, the same argument should apply in the cases of Mukhiyas, Pramukhs and Adhayakshas taking into account the total number of such posts in the whole State as provided for in Article 243D(4) of the Constitution. Hence, there is no contradiction between the order of the Patna High Court and the provisions of Article 243D(4) of Constitution which have been declared as a valid piece of law. The order of the Patna High Court will apply only if such post is a single one and not otherwise. The order of the Patna High Court should be read only in the context of the observation made by the Supreme Court that election will be held in accordance with the provision of "law as it stands today" and not in isolation. As the provisions of Article 243D(4) have been held as a valid piece of law, it is not clear to the Commission as to how an opposite view can be taken by the State government that reservation shall not apply for the post of Mukhiyas, Pramukhs and Adhayakshas by interpreting wrongly the expression "law as it stands today" used by Supreme Court in its order dated August 29, 2000.

(*vi*) The Supreme Court in its interim order dated August 29, 2000 in the SLP filed by the State government has clarified that the elections to the Panchayat can be held in accordance with "law as it stands today" which will be subject to the final decision in the pending appeal. In the order, the Supreme Court has not clarified "law" as it stands today, that is, whether the "law" stands for the above specific and mandatory provisions regarding reservation in

Article 243D(4) of the Constitution, or the Bihar Panchayat Raj Act, 1993 minus the manner (provisions) of reservation for the posts of Chairpersons in the Panchayats since the same has been quashed by the High Court at Patna. If the Patna High Court order dated March 19, 1996 is to be followed till final order of the Supreme Courts the provision of the Constitution providing reservation for the post of Chairperson in the Panchayat will have selective application in the country as other States have held Panchayat election with reservation for the posts of Chairpersons in favour of SC, ST and women while Bihar will be an exception. It is learnt that some High Court (M.P. for example) has upheld the Constitutional validity of reservation for the post of Chairperson in Panchayat as provided in the concerned State Panchayat Raj Act.

(*vii*) The State Election Commission is a Constitutional Body created under Article 243 K (1) of the Constitution and, therefore, it is under obligation to ensure that the provisions of the Constitution regarding elections to the Panchayats are not violated. As has been indicated above, the specific provisions regarding reservation against the posts of Mukhiyas, Pramukhs and Adhyakshas in favour of SC, ST and Women as provided for in Article 243 D(4) of the Constitution are still a valid piece of legislation and, therefore, the same, being a part of the Constitution, are inviolative. Commission is not, therefore, clear as to how being a Constitutional body mandated to uphold the provisions of the Constitution can conduct any election to the Panchayat without following the specific provisions of the Constitution regarding reservation against the posts of Chairpersons in the Panchayat Institutions.

Implication if No Clarification is given regarding Reservation to the Offices of Chairpersons in the Panchayat Institutions

Panchayat Institutions are the vehicles of political empowerment of people at the grassroots level for shaping their own destiny. A vast majority of people are living at the grassroots level in the rural and remote areas without any touch of modern day economic and social development. A large section of such a deprived people belong to SC and ST communities and other Backward Classes as also women in general at the grassroots level. Among the deprived section of the population at the grassroots level, the condition of the people belonging to the Scheduled Castes and the Scheduled Tribes is abysmally pathetic. In the Panchayat Institutions (grassroots level) which are embodiment of political empowerment of grassroots people, the offices of Chairpersons in the Panchayat at the village level or any other level is the most effective and decisive tool of the political empowerment in operation at grassroots level. Accordingly, mandatory provisions have been enshrined in Article 243D(4) of the Constitution reserving offices of Chairpersons for SC, ST and women in Panchayat Institutions at every level. Therefore, non-implementation of this mandatory and specific provision regarding reservation to the posts of Chairpersons in favour of SC, ST and women shall amount to negation of the constitutional scheme for grassroots democracy in real sense through the Institutions of Panchayat of which the Chairperson is the key figure. If a clarification is not given then as per the State government decision election to Panchayat will take place without any reservation to the offices of Chairpersons in favour of SC, ST and women in the Panchayat Institutions.

The Need for an Early Clarification

(*a*) The matter is very urgent as election to the offices of Chairperson (Mukhiya) at the Gram Panchayat level is direct. Sub-section (1) of Section 15 of the Bihar Panchayat Act, 1993 provides that Mukhiya shall be elected directly by the voters enrolled in the voters' list of the concerned Gram Panchayat. Therefore, election of Mukhiya shall have to be held also along with the election of Members of the Panchayats at all the three levels, i.e., Village, Block and District levels as a compulsion of administrative expediency and financial prudence.

(*b*) As against the direct election for the post of Mukhiya in the Gram Panchayat, the election of the Chairperson (Pramukh) for the Panchayat Samiti and Chairperson (Adhyaksha) for Zila Parishad is indirect. Section 38 and Section 65 of the Bihar Panchayat Raj Act, 1993 provides for election of Chairpersons of the Panchayat Samiti and Zila Parishad indirectly by the elected Members of the concerned Samiti/Zila parishad. The Supreme Court in its order dated August 29, 2000 has also observed that the election will be subject to final decision in the pending appeals. Thus in the event of the Supreme Court finally deciding that the post of Chairpersons shall be reserved for SC, ST and women there will not be any problem for electing persons belonging to SC and ST and also women as Chairpersons (Pramukh and Adhyaksha) as election to these posts is indirect and the elected Members of the Samiti and Zila Parishad can, anytime elect a reserved category of person as Chairperson by replacing the earlier elected general category candidate against a reserved post of Chairperson. However, as indicated earlier, such election for the post of Chairperson (Mukhiya) at the Gram Panchayat level will have to be held *de novo*. This will involve the same elaborate election process, like publication of voters' list, publication of polling stations, printing of ballot papers and conduct of actual election, i.e., filing of nomination papers, voting, counting etc. Apart from the strain on the administration and law and order problem, the expenditure will be enormous in conducting fresh election. Therefore, going by the constitutional mandate in Article 243D(4) regarding specific provision for reservation to the offices of Chairpersons in the Panchayat at every level for SC, ST and women, the balance of convenience lies in holding election to the post of Chairpersons in Panchayat in accordance with the above constitutional mandate regarding reservation for the posts of

Chairpersons (Mukhiyas) of the Gram Panchayat, where election is direct along with the current election process.

(*c*) The doubt and confusion in the mind of the State Election Commission, Bihar is genuine as the constitutional provisions regarding reservation to the offices of Chairpersons in the Panchayat system are applicable throughout the country and the State of Bihar cannot be an exception in their application. The process for holding election to Panchayat in Bihar has commenced since November 1, 2000. Hence, a clarification on the order of the Supreme Court dated August 29, 2000 is required before the statutory notification is issued by the Commission for the conduct of actual election, i.e., filing of nomination paper by the contestants, voting, counting, declaration of results etc. etc.

(*d*) No Court has so far declared that the Constitutional provisions under Article 243D(4) shall remain in abeyance till final decision by the court. The above provisions of the Constitution are applicable throughout the country and since the provisions have not been kept in abeyance by any competent court of law an early clarification on the doubt raised by the Commission as indicated above is essential.

Issues Involved

1. The State Election Commission, Bihar seeks clarification about the expression "law as it stands today" used by the Supreme Court in its order dated August 29, 2000 only on one issue, i.e., the election to the offices of Chairpersons only, in the Panchayat at village or any other level in accordance with specific provision in Article 243D(4) of the Constitution.
2. The doubt in the mind of the Commission on the questions of reservation for the posts of Mukhiyas, Pramukhs and Adhyakshas in favour of SC, ST and women is genuine.

The Doubt can be Clarified by Answering the Following Questions:

(*a*) Whether the provisions of Article 243D(4) regarding reservation for the posts of Chairpersons in the Panchayat Institutions for SC, ST and women are a valid piece of legislation or not? The answer is "Yes".

(*b*) Whether operation of the provisions of Article 243D(4) has been kept in abeyance by a competent court of law? The answer is "No."

(*c*) Whether the provisions of Article 243D(4) of the Constitution refers to the expression "Chairpersons" in the singular or in the plural form? The answer is "plural" ?

(*d*) Whether the number of each of the posts of Mukhiya, Pramukh and Adhyaksha in the State is one or more than one? The answer is "more than one."

(*e*) Whether the number of members in any constituency (Ward) under the jurisdiction of a Gram Panchayat or Panchayat Samiti or Zila Parishad is one or more than one? The answer is one and in that case a ward member also becomes a single post and, therefore, no reservation as per the Patna High Court order dated March 19, 1996. Therefore, there will be no reservation of any sort in the Panchayat, notwithstanding the mandatory provisions of Article 243D.

I did not get any support from the State government. The State government also did not argue the case in the Supreme Court when the IA filed by the Commission came up for hearing. It was somewhat unusual that the State government which had filed the SLP in the Apex Court against the order of the High Court on the same issue did not consider it proper to join the Commission in the IA. It was understood that the highest political authority was in favour of supporting the Commission in the Apex Court but the legal experts were of the view that it would amount to contempt of the Patna High Court. If the SLP filed by the State government did not amount to contempt how could an IA filed by the Commission for only a clarification of the interim order of the Apex Court dated August 29, 2000 become contempt. No wonder that with such legal luminaries of the State government the respondents in the SLP would not require any friendly advoc..tes.

The IA filed by the Commission came in for final hearing before the Apex Court on January 5, 2001. I was present in the court which dismissed the IA thus— "IAs are dismissed". No grounds for the dismissal were given. The State Government Standing Counsel in the Supreme Court made a silent appearance and left the Court in no time. The Solicitor General of India was to argue the case on behalf of Union of India but he did not open his mouth.

The Solicitor General of India whom I met earlier in this context gave me a very peculiar reasoning on the question of reservation for the posts of Chairpersons in the Panchayats. His argument was that since the Constitution provides for reservation by rotation the election should be conducted without reservation for the posts of Chairpersons. Such reservation could be given in the next round of election to the Panchayats. Thus according to the learned Solicitor General of India the spatial concept of rotation as per the provisions of the Constitution should be accorded a decent temporal burial. The Commission had no grudge against the Solicitor General of India for his legal opinion in the background of the opinion of the legal experts of the State government.

Thus Bihar has perhaps the singular distinction of being a State in the whole country where the constitutional provisions for reservation for the posts of Chairpersons of the Panchayats are not applicable. The reality, on the other hand, is that Bihar is one State where such reservation is absolutely essential.

Since the provisions for reservation of seats have not been quashed by any court it has been possible for the Commission to provide for the required reservation of seats *vide* Table 7.1, Table 7.2 and Table 7.3. In fact, actual reservation could be more than the prescribed percentage as the reservation has been provided Panchayat-wise and the Commission took the decision that if fraction of 1 is .5 or more it would be treated as 1 and where the fraction is less than .5 it could be ignored.

Table 7.1: Status of Reservation—Members of Gram Panchayat

Sl. No.	District	Scheduled Castes		Scheduled Tribes		*Unreserved		Total Post	
		Total	Female	Total	Female	Total	Female	Total	Female
1.	Patna	857	338	2	2	3699	1237	4558	1577
2.	Rohtas	620	249	17	12	2705	907	3342	1168
3.	Bhojpur	494	227	1	1	2619	876	3114	1104
4.	Nalanda	714	258	-	-	2686	904	3400	1162
5.	Buxar	271	138	-	-	1709	573	1980	711
6.	Kaimur	443	159	11	9	1448	481	1902	649
7.	Gaya	1491	495	-	-	3111	1048	4602	1543
8.	Nawada	639	212	1	1	1887	623	2527	836
9.	Aurangabad	680	226	-	-	2157	721	2837	947
10.	Jehanabad	418	162	-	-	1788	590	2206	752
11.	Saran	554	321	1	1	4129	1362	4684	1684
12.	Siwan	477	295	4	4	3605	1191	4086	1490
13.	Gopalganj	396	234	-	-	2797	930	3193	1164
14.	Muzaffarpur	874	393	-	-	4478	1495	5352	1888
15.	Vaishali	812	303	1	1	3200	1059	4013	1363
16.	E.Champaran	750	399	-	-	4936	1655	5686	2054
17.	W. Champaran	628	310	50	26	3541	1177	4219	1513
18.	Sitamarhi	451	263	-	-	3386	1125	3837	1388
19.	Sheohar	107	53	-	-	640	212	747	265
20.	Bhagalpur	319	212	88	47	2721	903	3128	1162
21.	Banka	298	172	124	65	2059	682	2481	919
22.	Madhubani	687	395	1	1	4828	1602	5516	1698
23.	Samastipur	948	386	-	-	4264	1424	5212	1810
24.	Darbhanga	679	333	-	-	3891	1306	4570	1998
25.	Saharsa	340	161	4	3	1760	578	2104	742
26.	Madhepura	371	170	13	10	1858	616	2242	796
27.	Supaul	394	188	5	5	2130	714	2529	907
28.	Purnia	440	217	139	89	2847	945	3426	1251
29.	Araria	411	190	30	24	2551	850	2992	1064
30.	Kishanganj	108	90	58	38	1603	527	1769	655
31.	Katihar	272	190	186	97	2815	939	3273	1226
32.	Munger	195	100	24	12	1144	381	1363	493
33.	Jamui	362	153	98	53	1503	513	1963	719
34.	Begusarai	522	255	-	-	2968	284	3490	539
35.	Khagaria	280	131	-	-	1579	525	1859	656
36.	Lakhisarai	191	81	8	5	916	308	1115	394
37.	Shekhpura	157	56	-	-	555	188	712	244
	Total	18650	8515	866	505	96513	31452	116029	40472

* Other than the seats reserved for S.C./S.T.

Table 7.2: Status of Reservation—Members of Panchayat Samiti

Sl. No.	District	Scheduled Castes		Scheduled Tribes		*Unreserved		Total Post	
		Total	Female	Total	Female	Total	Female	Total	Female
1.	Patna	84	31	-	-	370	123	454	154
2.	Rohtas	60	24	2	2	268	88	330	114
3.	Bhojpur	47	15	-	-	263	89	310	104
4.	Nalanda	71	27	-	-	271	90	342	117
5.	Buxar	27	11	-	-	173	60	200	71
6.	Kaimur	42	14	3	1	147	47	192	62
7.	Gaya	150	50	-	-	310	105	460	155
8.	Nawada	65	21	-	-	189	63	254	84
9.	Aurangabad	69	24	-	-	216	72	285	96
10.	Jehanabad	41	14	-	-	181	60	222	74
11.	Saran	55	21	-	-	414	136	469	157
12.	Siwan	48	17	-	-	363	120	411	137
13.	Gopalganj	39	15	-	-	283	95	322	110
14.	Muzaffarpur	87	28	-	-	448	149	535	177
15.	Vaishali	80	25	-	-	319	106	399	131
16.	E. Champaran	77	33	-	-	494	166	571	199
17.	W. Champaran	61	24	5	2	355	119	421	145
18.	Sitamarhi	45	20	-	-	339	113	384	133
19.	Sheohar	10	5	-	-	62	20	72	25
20.	Bhagalpur	32	16	9	4	273	90	314	110
21.	Banka	29	11	12	6	209	70	250	87
22.	Madhubani	68	24	-	-	477	157	545	181
23.	Samastipur	94	30	-	-	428	144	522	174
24.	Darbhanga	71	23	-	-	388	130	459	153
25.	Saharsa	33	12	-	-	176	58	209	70
26.	Madhepura	35	14	1	1	189	62	225	77
27.	Supaul	42	15	-	-	213	71	255	86
28.	Purnia	45	19	15	9	286	98	346	126
29.	Araria	43	15	4	3	256	84	303	102
30.	Kishanganj	11	7	6	3	159	52	176	62
31.	Katihar	28	16	19	13	282	92	329	121
32.	Munger	20	9	3	2	113	38	136	49
33.	Jamui	35	12	11	7	147	48	193	67
34.	Begusarai	51	19	-	-	297	99	348	118
35.	Khagaria	29	10	-	-	156	52	185	62
36.	Lakhisarai	20	8	1	1	92	31	113	40
37.	Shekhpura	15	6	-	-	55	18	70	24
	Total	1859	685	91	54	9661	3215	11611	3954

* Other than the seats reserved for S.C./S.T.

Table 7.3: Status of Reservation—Members of Zila Parishad

Sl. No.	*District*	*Scheduled Castes*		*Scheduled Tribes*		**Unreserved*		*Total Post*	
		Total	*Female*	*Total*	*Female*	*Total*	*Female*	*Total*	*Female*
1.	Patna	9	3	-	-	37	12	46	15
2.	Rohtas	6	2	-	-	27	9	33	11
3.	Bhojpur	5	2	-	-	26	9	31	11
4.	Nalanda	7	2	-	-	27	9	34	11
5.	Buxar	3	1	-	-	17	6	20	7
6.	Kaimur	4	1	-	-	15	5	19	6
7.	Gaya	15	5	-	-	31	10	46	15
8.	Nawada	6	2	-	-	19	6	25	8
9.	Aurangabad	7	2	-	-	21	7	28	9
10.	Jehanabad	4	1	-	-	18	6	22	7
11.	Saran	6	2	-	-	41	14	47	16
12.	Siwan	5	2	-	-	36	12	41	14
13.	Gopalganj	4	1	-	-	28	9	32	10
14.	Muzaffarpur	9	3	-	-	45	15	54	18
15.	Vaishali	8	3	-	-	33	11	41	14
16.	E.Champaran	8	3	-	-	49	16	57	19
17.	W. Champaran	6	2	1	1	35	12	42	15
18.	Sitamarhi	4	1	-	-	34	11	38	12
19.	Sheohar	1	1	-	-	6	2	7	3
20.	Bhagalpur	3	1	1	1	27	9	31	11
21.	Banka	3	1	1	1	21	7	25	9
22.	Madhubani	7	2	-	-	49	16	56	18
23.	Samastipur	9	3	-	-	42	14	51	17
24.	Darbhanga	7	2	-	-	40	13	47	15
25.	Saharsa	3	1	-	-	18	6	21	7
26.	Madhepura	4	1	-	-	19	6	23	7
27.	Supaul	4	1	-	-	21	7	25	8
28.	Purnia	4	1	2	1	28	9	34	11
29.	Araria	4	1	-	-	26	9	30	10
30.	Kishanganj	1	1	1	1	16	5	18	7
31.	Katihar	3	1	2	1	28	9	33	11
32.	Munger	2	1	-	-	12	4	14	5
33.	Jamui	4	1	1	1	15	5	20	7
34.	Begusarai	5	2	-	-	30	10	35	12
35.	Khagaria	3	1	-	-	15	5	18	6
36.	Lakhisarai	2	1	-	-	9	3	11	4
37.	Shekhpura	2	1	-	-	5	2	7	3
	Total	187	62	9	7	966	320	1162	389

* Other than the seats reserved for S.C./S.T.

Even though there was no reservation for the offices of Chairpersons of the Panchayats, many candidates belonging to the Scheduled Castes and the Scheduled Tribes contested for the posts of Chairpersons (Mukhiya, Pramukh and Adhyaksha) and some of them got elected to such posts vide Table 7.4 below:

Table 7.4

Name of the Post	*Total Number of posts*	*Minimum No. Admissible*		*Actual Achievement*	
		S.C.	*S.T.*	*S.C.*	*S.T.*
Mukhiya	8471	1317	80	143	39
Pramukh	529	85	3	36	1
Adhyaksha	37	6	0	0	0

It will be quite pertinent here to specially mention the golden opportunity that the State lost in the empowerment of women. Table 7.5 below would give a very pathetic picture of admissible number of Chairpersons in favour of women as mandated by the Constitution and the actual achievement. As against the minimum number of posts of 2824 Mukhiya, the kingpin in the Panchayat system, the actual number won by women was a dismal 78. It speaks volumes for the concern shown by the political leadership for emancipation of women.

Table 7.5

Name of the Post	*Total Number of Posts*	*Minimum Number Admissible for Women*	*Actual Achievement*
Mukhiya	8471	2824	78
Pramukh	529	176	54
Adhyaksha	37	12	9

I have repeatedly emphasized the importance of Mukhiya of the Gram Panchayat in Bihar. Even if we ignore, for the time being, the representation of the Scheduled Castes and the Scheduled Tribes in the offices of the Chairpersons of the Panchayats specially the Gram Panchayat, one should not ignore the importance of woman Chairperson of Gram Panchayat in Bihar as this would have made a sea-change in the rural areas. In this context I would refer to two of my personal experiences below.

Immediately after my assuming the charge of State Election Commissioner there was a meeting of Divisional Commissioners and the District Magistrates of undivided Bihar in the first week of November, 2000 addressed by the Chief Minister. The meeting was convened as a follow-up of the decision of the government to conduct election to the Panchayats. All the Divisional Commissioners and the District Magistrates, specially the women officers, strongly pleaded that if the posts of Chairpersons of the Panchayats were not reserved for the Scheduled Castes, the Scheduled Tribes and women it would be violation of the constitutional mandate. As I was sitting on the dais next to the Chief Minister she asked me if what the officers were saying was correct. I told her that the officers were right. Taking the advantage of a woman Chief Minister I specifically conveyed that there would be no reservation for the post of Mukhiya in favour of women even though the State had a woman Chief Minister. The immediate reaction of the Chief Minister was that if there could be no reservation for the post of Mukhiya in favour of women *Chunao Bekar Ho Jayega* (the entire election will be meaningless).

She was quite upset and whispered to me that I should meet "Saheb" (her husband Sri Laloo Yadav) in the evening itself when she would also be present to discuss the issue so that reservation for the posts of Chairpersons of the Panchayats, specially the post of Mukhiya, in favour of women, could be ensured. I was quite excited and hopeful that the Chief Minister, being a pious and simple person, would definitely succeed in the matter. In the evening I tried to ascertain from C.M. Secretariat the convenient time for the meeting. I was advised first to discuss the matter with her Principal Secretary. The message was that I should forget the matter. It was not a volte-face on the part of the Chief Minister as she is incapable of being dishonest on such a vital issue so close to her heart. She knows fully well the importance and relevance of a woman Mukhiya in changing the face of women in general in rural Bihar.

I must here refer to the most pathetic role of women organizations in the State which failed miserably in taking advantage of a woman Chief Minister in ensuring reservation for the posts of Chairpersons in Panchayats. A small delegation of women representing some organizations had called on me two three times on the eve of election to the Panchayats and vowed to take up the cause with all seriousness. But I think their mission was over after giving a press statement which was published in some print media. It is a sad reflection on the State which had many women ministers, both in State Cabinet and Union Cabinet in the past, that no woman leader raised any voice against non-compliance with the constitutional mandate for reservation in favour of women for the posts of Chairpersons of the Panchayats.

There was yet another incident when some newspapers reported wrongly that the election of the father of the Chief Minister as Mukhiya of a Gram Panchayat in her native district was illegal. I got a message that the Chief Minister was worried about this news item. I assured the officer concerned that there was nothing to worry and a decision on merit could be taken. It was altogether a different matter that there was nothing illegal against the election.

I am referring to these incidents only to highlight the importance attached to the post of Mukhiya of a Gram Panchayat even by the highest political authority in the State which is also the general perception in the rural areas. One could draw his own conclusion whether representation of the disadvantaged section of the society should be there or not for the offices of Chairpersons of the Panchayats, specially of the Gram Panchayat.

The State government had taken the plea that in view of the order of the Patna High Court dated March 19, 1996 the gvernment was not in a position to provide for reservation in the offices of Chairpersons of the Panchayats. If we look at the legal aspect it would be very clear that the Constitution and the Act only provides for certain number of posts to be reserved for certain categories of persons and that is the minimum number under the law while the political leadership could always on their own earmark certain number of offices of Chairpersons in the Panchayat for the reserved categories of persons. Moreover, no court had, so far, quashed the constitutional provisions of reservations for the offices of Chairpersons of the Panchayats. Thus, there was no bar under the law to ensure representation of the reserved categories of persons in the offices of Chairpersons of the Panchayats and by doing so they could prove their *bona fides* rather than taking the embargo under the High Court order as the Court would not have interfered if the political leadership could make an informal understanding on the issue. The argument that the election to the Panchayats was held on non-party basis and, therefore, the political parties could not have intervened in the matter would not cut ice as immediately after election important political functionaries have indirectly hinted and reported by the newspapers the number of persons belonging to certain backward castes elected as Chairpersons of the Panchayats at each level. In the context of Bihar remote but effective role of the political leadership in ensuring the victory of their respective caste-men to the offices of Chairpersons of the Panchayats at different levels is a matter of fact. If we look at the personal profile of the elected Chairpersons of the Panchayats in Table 8.1, Table 8.2 and Table 8.3 in Chapter 8, we could see an impressive number of offices of Chairpersons cornered by a particular section of the population without any mandatory backing of the Constitution compared to the pathetic scenario for the people for whom the constitutional mandate provides for reservation. This will be dealt with in Chapter 8.

Reservation in the Municipalities

In the preceding paragraphs I have dealt with the issue of reservation of seats and Chairpersons in the Panchayats. Similar constitutional provisions have been made for the

Municipalities under Article 243-T of the Constitution, which is extracted below:

243-T. Reservation of Seats

1. Seats shall be reserved for the Scheduled Castes and the Scheduled Tribes in every municipality and the number of seats so reserved shall bear, as nearly as may be, the same proportion to the total number of seats to be filled by direct election in that municipality as the population of the Scheduled Castes in the municipal area or of the Scheduled Tribes in the municipal area bears to the total population of that area and such seats may be allotted by rotation to different constituencies in a municipality.
2. Not less than one-third of the total number of seats reserved under clause (1) shall be reserved for women belonging to the Scheduled Castes or as the case may be, the Scheduled Tribes.
3. Not less than one-third (including the number of seats reserved for women belonging to the Scheduled Castes and the Scheduled Tribes) of the total number of seats to be filled by direct election in every municipality shall be reserved for women and such seats may be allotted by rotation to different constituencies in a municipality.
4. The offices of Chairpersons in the municipalities shall be reserved for the Scheduled Castes, the Scheduled Tribes and women in such manner as the legislature of a State may, by law, provide.
5. The reservation of seats under clauses (1) and (2) and the reservation of offices of Chairpersons (other than the reservation for women) under clause (4) shall cease to have effect on the expiration of the period specified in Article 334.
6. Nothing in this Part shall prevent the Legislature of a State from making any provision for reservation of seats in any municipality or offices of Chairpersons

in the municipalities in favour of backward class of citizens.

It will be seen that as in the case of Panchayats, in municipalities also posts of ward commissioner/councillor would be reserved for the Scheduled Castes, the Scheduled Tribes and women and the number of seats to be reserved shall be proportionate to the population belonging to the above castes. As regards reservation for women, the provision is identical in respect of the Panchayats and the municipalities according to which not less than one-third of the total number of seats shall be reserved for women including women belonging to the Scheduled Castes and the Scheduled Tribes.

There is a difference between the provisions relating to reservations of the offices of Chairpersons of the Panchayats and those of the municipalities. Thus while clause (4) of Article 243D prescribes the manner in which the number of offices of Chairpersons of the Panchayats to be reserved for the Scheduled Castes, the Scheduled Tribes and women should be calculated, clause (4) of Article 243T leaves it to the State Legislature to make appropriate provisions. As regards the duration in reservation of seats (wards) in favour of the Scheduled Castes and the Scheduled Tribes the farthest limit of the period shall be the same as prescribed under Article 334 except that reservation in favour of women would be a permanent feature of the Constitution.

As in the case of Article 243D, an identical provision has been made under Article 243T with an enabling provision for reservation in favour of Backward Class of citizens. The two Acts (the Bihar Act and the Patna Act) enacted by the State Legislature have provisions for reservation in the municipalities. The relevant sections, i.e., Section 8(2) of the Patna Act and Section 13(3) of the Bihar Act are extracted below:

8 (2) (*a*) Seats of Municipal Councillors shall be reserved for the Scheduled Castes, Scheduled Tribes and Backward Classes in the Corporation and the number

of seats so reserved shall bear, as nearly as may be, the same proportion to the total number of seats to be filled in by direct election in the Corporation as the population of the Scheduled Castes, Scheduled Tribes or of Backward Classes in the Corporation area bears to the total population of that area, and such seats shall be allotted by rotation to different constituencies in Corporation in such manner as may be prescribed by the State Election Commission.

(*b*) Not less than one-third of the total number of seats reserved under clause (a) shall be reserved for women belonging to the Scheduled Castes, the Scheduled Tribes and the Backward Classes, as the case may be.

(*c*) Not less than one-third (including the number of seats reserved for women belonging to the Scheduled Castes, the Scheduled Tribes and the Backward Classes) of total number of seats to be filled in by direct election in the Corporation shall be reserved for women and such seats may be allotted by rotation to different constituencies in the Corporation in such manner, as may be prescribed.

Explanation—For the removal of doubts it is hereby declared that the principle of rotation for the purposes of reservation under this sub-section shall commence from the first election to be held after the commencement of this Ordinance.

(*d*) The reservation of seats under clauses (a) and (b) shall cease to have effect on the expiration of the period specified in Article 334 of Constitution of India:

Provided that the reservation of seats under clause (a), (b) and (c) shall be made by the District Magistrate under the direction, control and supervision of the State Election Commission.

13 (3) (*a*) Seats shall be reserved for the Scheduled Castes, Scheduled Tribes and Backward Classes in every

municipality and the number of seats so reserved shall bear, as nearly as may be the same proportion to the total number of seats to be filled in by direct election in that municipality as the population of the Scheduled Castes, the Scheduled Tribes or Backward Classes in the municipal area bears to the population of that area, and such seats may be allotted by rotation to different constituencies in a municipality by the District Magistrate under the direction, control and supervision of the State Election Commission.

(*b*) Not less than one-third of the total number of seats reserved under clause (a) of this sub-section, shall be reserved for women belonging to the Scheduled Castes or the Scheduled Tribes or Backward Classes as the case may be.

(*c*) Not less than one-third (including the number of seats reserved for women belonging to the Scheduled Castes, Scheduled Tribes and Backward Classes) of the total number of seats to be filled in by direct election in every municipality shall be reserved for women and such seats may be allotted by rotation to different constituencies in a municipality in such manner as may be prescribed.

(*d*) The office of the Chairman in municipalities shall be reserved in the following manner:

(*i*) Such number of offices of Chairman of the municipality in the State shall be reserved for persons belonging to the Scheduled Castes, Scheduled Tribes and Backward Classes bearing, as nearly as may be the same proportion to the total number of offices in the State as the population of the Scheduled Castes, the Scheduled Tribes and the Backward Classes in the State bears to the total population of the State, and

(*ii*) Not less than one-third of the total offices of the Chairman in the State shall be reserved for women, but not less than one-third of offices of the Chairman in the State reserved under clause (i) shall be reserved for women belonging to the Scheduled Castes, Scheduled Tribes and Backward Classes, as the case may be:

Provided that the offices reserved under this clause shall be allotted by rotation to different municipalities by the State Election Commission.

Explanation—For the removal of doubts it is hereby declared that the principle of rotation for the purposes of reservation of offices under this sub-section shall commence from the first election to be held after the commencement of this Ordinance.

(*e*) The reservation of seats under clause (a) and (b) and the reservation of office of Chairman (other than the reservation of women) under clause (d) shall cease to have effect on the expiration of the period specified in Article 334 of the Constitution of India.

If we go through the relevant provisions of the above two sections it will be seen that seats as well as the offices of Chairpersons shall be reserved for the Scheduled Castes, the Scheduled Tribes and Backward Classes and women in the municipalities, while for the Corporation only seats shall be reserved for the above categories of persons and that the offices of Chairpersons shall not be so reserved. The rationale behind discrimination between the Corporation and the municipalities with reference to the offices of Chairpersons is not clear. No reservation could be provided for Backward Classes in election to the Urban Local Bodies as the above two Acts do not contain the list of Backward Classes separately. The Acts only provide that Backward Classes shall be the same as listed in Schedule-I of the Panchayat Act. Since Schedule-I of the Panchayat Act was quashed by the Patna High Court referred to earlier, no reservation could be given to Backward Classes in the absence of a legally valid list of

Backward classes even though the two Acts relating to municipalities have a provision to that effect.

Elections to the municipalities were conducted and seats as well as the offices of Chairpersons were reserved for the Scheduled Castes, the Scheduled Tribes and women in the municipalities. As far as the five Municipal Corporations were concerned only the seats could be reserved.

On the request of the State government the Commission announced a schedule for election of the Mayors and the Deputy Mayors (Chairpersons and Vice-Chairpersons) of the five Municipal Corporations. While the date for the election of the Mayors and the Deputy Mayors were nearing, the State government became unusually active and a request was made to the Commission that election schedule for the Mayors and the Deputy Mayors of the Corporations be deferred as the State government proposed to make provisions in the Patna Act for reserving the offices of Mayors in the Municipal Corporations for the Scheduled Castes, the Scheduled Tribes and women as mandated by the Constitution. I got some urgent telephonic requests also for deferring the election. Since the election of Mayors and the Deputy Mayors are indirect, i.e., they are to be elected by the directly elected ward councillors and the request of the State government was to comply with the constitutional mandate, I agreed to the request of the State government and deferred the election schedule.

The State government subsequently inserted a new section, i.e., Section 19A in the Patna Municipal Corporation Act, 1951. The above section is reproduced below:

19 A. The offices of the Mayors in the Municipal Corporations of the State shall be reserved in the following manner:

(*i*) The proportion of reserved numbers of offices of Mayors of the Municipal Corporations in the State shall be for persons belonging to the Scheduled Castes and the Scheduled Tribes, as nearly as may be, the same which proportion of the Scheduled

Castes and the Scheduled Tribes is in the total population of the State.

(*ii*) Not less than one-third of the total offices of the Mayors in the Municipal Corporation of the State shall be reserved for women.

(*iii*) At least one-third of the total offices reserved under clause (i) shall be filled from amongst women belonging to Scheduled Castes and Scheduled Tribes, as the case may be:

Provided that the offices reserved under this clause shall be allotted by rotation by the State Election Commission to different Municipal Corporations in such manner as may be prescribed.

Explanation—For the removal of doubts it is hereby explained that for the purpose of offices reserved under this new clause the principle of rotation shall come into effect from the first election to be held after the commencement of this Act:

Provided further that the reservation of the offices of Mayors under clauses (i), (ii) and (iii) (other than the reservation for women) shall cease to have effect on the expiration of the period specified in Article 334 of the Constitution of India.

Thus with the insertion of a new section in the Patna Act as quoted above, the constitutional mandate of reservation of seats and reservation of offices of Chairpersons in the Municipalities, i.e., Municipal Corporation, Nagar Parishad and Nagar Panchayat, has been complied with. I have stated earlier that seats as well as offices of Chairperson have been reserved for the Nagar Parishad and the Nagar Panchayat as per the provisions of the Bihar Act. However, only seats could be reserved for the Municipal Corporations. With the amendment in the Patna Act reservation of offices of Chairperson, i.e., Mayor, in the Municipal Corporations have also been provided and two posts of Mayor have been reserved for the Scheduled Castes, the Scheduled Tribes and women and in the first rotation both the posts have gone in favour of woman, one in favour of a Scheduled Caste woman and the other in favour of a general category woman. The following three tables, *i.e.*, Table 7.6, Table 7.7 and Table 7.8 would give the details of reservation of seats in the five Municipal Corporations, 32 Nagar Parishads and 80 Nagar Panchayats respectively:

Table 7.6: Status of Reservation of Seats—Municipal Corporation

Sl. No.	*Municipal Corporation*	*Scheduled Castes*		*Scheduled Tribes*		**Unreserved*		*Total Posts*	
		Total	*Female*	*Total*	*Female*	*Total*	*Female*	*Total*	*Female*
1.	Patna	5	2	0	0	52	17	57	19
2.	Gaya	4	1	0	0	36	12	40	13
3.	Bhagalpur	3	1	0	0	35	12	38	13
4.	Muzaffarpur	3	1	0	0	35	12	38	13
5.	Darbhanga	4	1	0	0	33	11	37	12
	Total	19	6	0	0	191	64	210	70

* Other than the seats reserved for S.C./S.T.

Table 7.7: Status of Reservation of Seats—Nagar Parishad

Sl. No.	*Nagar Parishad*	*Scheduled Castes*		*Scheduled Tribes*		**Unreserved*		*Total Posts*	
		Total	*Female*	*Total*	*Female*	*Total*	*Female*	*Total*	*Female*
1.	Barh	3	1	0	0	19	6	22	7
2.	Khagaul	3	1	0	0	19	6	22	7
3.	Danapur	3	1	0	0	25	8	28	9
4.	Mokamah	4	1	0	0	20	7	24	8
5.	Arrah	3	1	0	0	32	11	35	12
6.	Buxar	2	1	0	0	22	7	24	8
7.	Sasaram	2	1	0	0	28	9	30	10
8.	Dehri Dalmia-nagar	3	1	0	0	27	9	30	10
9.	Biharsharif	3	1	0	0	34	11	37	12
10.	Jchanabad	3	1	0	0	21	7	24	8
11.	Aurangabad	3	1	0	0	19	6	22	7
12.	Nawada	2	1	0	0	22	7	24	8
13.	Sitamarhi	1	1	0	0	21	7	22	8
14.	Hajipur	5	2	0	0	23	8	28	10

(*Contd.*)

TABLE 7.7 (*Contd.*)

Sl. No.	Nagar Parishad	Scheduled Castes		Scheduled Tribes		*Unreserved		Total Posts	
		Total	Female	Total	Female	Total	Female	Total	Female
15.	Motihari	2	1	0	0	26	9	28	10
16.	Betiah	2	1	0	0	28	9	30	10
17.	Bagha	2	1	0	0	24	8	26	9
18.	Madhubani	2	1	0	0	22	7	24	8
19.	Samastipur	3	1	0	0	21	7	24	8
20.	Munger	2	1	0	0	33	11	35	12
21.	Jamalpur	3	1	0	0	25	8	28	9
22.	Lakhisarai	3	1	0	0	21	7	24	8
23.	Jamui	3	1	0	0	19	6	22	7
24.	Begusarai	3	1	0	0	23	8	26	9
25.	Chapra	3	1	0	0	31	10	34	11
26.	Siwan	2	1	0	0	26	9	28	10
27.	Saharsa	3	1	0	0	25	8	28	9
28.	Supaul	2	1	0	0	20	7	22	8
29.	Purnia	3	1	1	1	28	9	32	11
30.	Araria	2	1	0	0	20	7	22	8
31.	Kishanganj	3	1	0	0	23	8	26	9
32.	Katihar	3	1	0	0	32	11	35	12
	Total	86	33	1	1	779	258	866	292

* Other than the seats reserved for S.C./S.T.

Table 7.8: Status of Reservation of Seats—Nagar Panchayats

Sl. No.	Nagar Panchayats	Scheduled Castes		Scheduled Tribes		*Unreserved		Total Posts	
		Total	Female	Total	Female	Total	Female	Total	Female
1.	Fatuha	3	1	0	0	15	5	18	6
2.	Masaurhi	2	1	0	0	16	5	18	6
3.	Maner	2	1	0	0	12	4	14	5
4.	Fulwarisharif	2	1	0	0	18	6	20	7
5.	Bakhtiyarpur	3	1	0	0	13	4	16	5
6.	Piro	1	1	0	0	11	4	12	5
7.	Bihian	1	1	0	0	11	4	12	5
8.	Jagdishpur	1	1	0	0	13	4	14	5
9.	Dumraon	2	1	0	0	16	5	18	6
10.	Bikramganj	2	1	0	0	14	5	16	6
11.	Koath	2	1	0	0	8	3	10	4

(*Contd.*)

TABLE 7.8 (*Contd.*)

Sl. No.	Nagar Panchayats	Scheduled Castes		Scheduled Tribes		*Unreserved		Total Posts	
		Total	Female	Total	Female	Total	Female	Total	Female
12.	Nokha	2	1	0	0	10	3	12	4
13.	Nasriganj	1	1	0	0	11	4	12	5
14.	Hilsa	2	1	0	0	14	5	16	6
15.	Islampur	1	1	0	0	13	4	14	5
16.	Silaw	2	1	0	0	10	3	12	4
17.	Rajgir	4	1	0	0	10	4	14	5
18.	Bhabhua	2	1	0	0	14	5	16	6
19.	Bodh Gaya	4	1	0	0	10	4	14	5
20.	Sherghati	3	1	0	0	13	4	16	5
21.	Tekari	1	1	0	0	9	3	10	4
22.	Makhdumpur	3	1	0	0	11	4	14	5
23.	Rafiganj	2	1	0	0	10	3	12	4
24.	Nawinagar	2	1	0	0	8	3	10	4
25.	Daudnagar	2	1	0	0	16	5	18	6
26.	Warsaliganj	2	1	0	0	12	4	14	5
27.	Hisua	2	1	0	0	10	3	12	4
28.	Nawgachhia	1	1	0	0	17	6	18	7
29.	Sultanganj	1	1	0	0	17	6	18	7
30.	Kahalgaon	1	1	0	0	11	4	12	5
31.	Banka	2	1	0	0	14	5	16	6
32.	Amarpur	1	1	0	0	11	4	12	5
33.	Bargania	2	1	0	0	14	5	16	6
34.	Belsand	1	1	0	0	9	3	10	4
35.	Sheohar	2	1	0	0	8	3	10	4
36.	Motipur	2	1	0	0	10	3	12	4
37.	Kanti	3	1	0	0	9	3	12	4
38.	Lalganj	2	1	0	0	12	4	14	5
39.	Mahnar	4	1	0	0	14	5	18	6
40.	Chakiya	1	1	0	0	9	3	10	4
41.	Sugauli	1	1	0	0	13	4	14	5
42.	Dhaka	1	1	0	0	13	4	14	5
43.	Areraj	1	1	0	0	9	3	10	4
44.	Raxaul	1	1	0	0	15	5	16	6
45.	Chanpatia	1	1	0	0	11	4	12	5
46.	Narkatiaganj	2	1	0	0	16	5	18	6
47.	Ramnagar	2	1	0	0	14	5	16	6
48.	Jaynagar	2	1	0	0	10	3	12	4
49.	Jhanjharpur	2	1	0	0	12	4	14	5

(*Contd.*)

TABLE 7.8 (*Contd.*)

Sl. No.	*Nagar Panchayats*	*Scheduled Castes*		*Scheduled Tribes*		**Unreserved*		*Total Posts*	
		Total	*Female*	*Total*	*Female*	*Total*	*Female*	*Total*	*Female*
50.	Ghoghardiha	1	1	0	0	9	3	10	4
51.	Dalsinghsarai	3	1	0	0	9	3	12	4
52.	Rosra	2	1	0	0	12	4	14	5
53.	Haweli Kharagpur	3	1	0	0	13	4	16	5
54.	Barahiya	1	1	0	0	17	6	18	7
55.	Jhajha	2	1	0	0	16	5	18	6
56.	Shekhpura	3	1	0	0	15	5	18	6
57.	Barbigha	3	1	0	0	15	5	18	6
58.	Khagaria	1	1	0	0	17	6	18	7
59.	Gogri Jamalpur	1	1	0	0	13	4	14	5
60.	Sonepur	2	1	0	0	14	5	16	6
61.	Dighwara	2	1	0	0	12	4	14	5
62.	Madhora	2	1	0	0	12	4	14	5
63.	Rivilganj	2	1	0	0	14	5	16	6
64.	Maharajganj	1	1	0	0	11	4	12	5
65.	Mairwa	1	1	0	0	9	3	10	4
66.	Gopalganj	2	1	0	0	18	6	20	7
67.	Mirganj	1	1	0	0	11	4	12	5
68.	Barauli	1	1	0	0	15	5	16	6
69.	Karaiya	2	1	0	0	8	3	10	4
70.	Birpur	1	1	0	0	9	3	10	4
71.	Nirmali	1	1	0	0	9	3	10	4
72.	Madhepura	1	1	0	0	17	6	18	7
73.	Murliganj	2	1	0	0	12	4	14	5
74.	Kaswa	1	1	0	0	13	4	14	5
75.	Banmankhi	1	1	0	0	13	4	14	5
76.	Jogwani	2	1	0	0	12	4	14	5
77.	Farwishganj	1	1	0	0	17	6	18	7
78.	Bahadurganj	1	1	0	0	13	4	14	5
79.	Thakurganj	1	1	0	0	9	3	10	4
80.	Manihari	3	1	0	0	9	3	12	4
	Total	143	80	0	0	989	333	1132	413

* Other than the seats reserved for S.C./S.T.

Table 7.9 would give the number of offices of Chairperson reserved for the Scheduled Castes, the Scheduled Tribes and the women in Municipal Corporations, Nagar Parishads and Nagar Panchayats:

Table 7.9: Status of Reservation of Chairpersons—Municipalities

Sl. No.	*Municipalities*	*Scheduled Castes*		*Scheduled Tribes*		**Unreserved*		*Total Post*	
		Total	*Female*	*Total*	*Female*	*Total*	*Female*	*Total*	*Female*
1. Municipal Corporation	5	1	1	0	0	4	1	5	2
2. Nagar Parishad	32	5	2	0	0	27	9	32	11
3. Nagar Panchayat	80	12	4	0	0	68	23	80	15

* Other than the seats reserved for S.C./S.T.

Thus in so far as the municipalities are concerned the constitutional mandate of reservation of seats and offices of chairpersons has been fully complied with.

After the elections to the Panchayats and the municipalities were over I was pondering over the question why the State government remained so indifferent to the question of reservation in the offices of Chairpersons of the Panchayats. Such an indifferent attitude of the State government was quite baffling in the context of its overenthusiasm for reservation in the offices of Chairpersons in the Municipal Corporation.

I made an attempt to probe the matter informally through discussions with some well-informed persons including some senior bureaucrats who have interests in the matter. Everybody agrees that Bihar is a fit case for politically empowering the downtrodden sections of society, and women in general in the rural areas, for any meaningful economic development. In course of my discussions with these persons certain facts emerged which are quite revealing. I will sum up the opinion so gathered below.

Schedule I to the Act contained a list of 129 backward castes. This list also includes some castes which, according to the Patna High Court judgement of March 19, 1996, do not deserve any reservation. The High Court had quashed Schedule I and suggested amendment of the Schedule. Empirical evidence as reflected in the result of the elections to the Panchayats and the municipalities indicates that the predominant castes among the backward castes have cornered more than 50 per cent of the total posts including the posts of Chairpersons both in the PRIs and ULBs while the total population of these castes may not exceed 15 per cent of the total population of the State. It is, therefore, clear that if the other backward castes (excluding the 3 or 4 predominant backward castes) are to be given proportionate representation for seats and the offices of Chairpersons in PRIs and ULBs, the political apple-cart of the ruling class would get upset. It is, therefore, advisable that these "other" backward castes are not allowed to realize that their numerical strength is enough to take over the leadership of not only the grassroots institutions of self-governance but they can also be a strong force to reckon with at the State level. Though I am not an expert on such vexed social issues, the fact that some well-meaning persons entertain the above opinion is worth deliberating further by social scientists.

In this context it will be worthwhile to understand the significance of the judgement of the Patna High Court dated March 19, 1996. The Court had not quashed the provisions of reservations of seats for the backward castes except that number of reserved seats shall not exceed 50 per cent of the total seats. The Court has suggested deletion of certain castes from the list of backward castes included in Schedule I of the Act. There is no denying the fact that many backward castes are economically extremely poor except that persons belonging to such extremely poor backward castes are not untouchable like the Scheduled Castes irrespective of their economic status. Therefore, the reason for not extending the benefit of reservation of seats to certain disadvantaged sections among the backward castes is not clear.

As regards the question of reservation for the offices of Chairpersons of Panchayats, the Court had come to the conclusion that it is a single post and hence reservation is not permissible. Whether the High Court is right or not in declaring the posts of Chairpersons as single is to be decided by the Supreme Court in the SLP filed by the State government.

While discussing the question of reservation of seats in favour of the backward castes, I asked whether the logic would not apply to the case of the Scheduled Castes also as the benefit of reservation in their case has also been cornered by only a few castes among the Scheduled Castes. Same is the case for the Scheduled Tribes also. They admitted that such a possibility could be there also. But their argument was that such controversy would only deny the legitimate claims of the extremely poor among the backward castes for reservation in the PRIs at the grassroots level where most of such people live. In other words, a debate on such a complex social issue would only delay a decision indefinitely.

8

Personal Profile of the Elected Representatives of the Panchayats

I have narrated the challenges and the shortage of time I had to face in organizing the entire election machinery for the conduct of election to the Panchayats. We have seen that the number of contesting candidates whose nominations were finally accepted was 4,36,232. If we take into account the likely number of nominations rejected during scrutiny and the number of nominations withdrawn after scrutiny this figure could perhaps touch 600,000. For want of time and also due to lack of experience on the part of the Returning Officers I could not make it mandatory to collect certain relevant data that should also have gone into the personal profile of the persons filing nomination. If it was made mandatory every person filing nomination would have been required to submit the required details in a separate annexure. In retrospect I realized that my omission was not without any positive aspects as it would have been very difficult for the Returning Officers to ensure its compliance.

Subsequently the Commission compiled the details about the chairpersons of the Gram Panchayat, Panchayat Samiti and Zila Parishad. I have deliberately left out such details about the members of the Gram Panchayat whose number is 1,16,029 and it would have been a very difficult task to collect necessary information about such a large number of persons within a reasonable time. The same is the case with members of Panchayat Samitis and members of Zila Parishads.

Relevant information to be collected, included age, educational qualification, gender and caste of the elected chairpersons of the Panchayats. For selecting the above items I have gone by my own logic. Going by the enthusiasm shown by the younger generation of the people who were meeting me in large numbers as also the keen interest taken by the women I thought it necessary to get the age and gender profile of the elected representatives. Likewise, a large number of educated persons were found to be quite active during election and, therefore, I thought that we must also have an idea about the educational profile of these persons.

The last item is caste which, no doubt, would look somewhat anachronistic in the present electronic age but in the context of the social fabric of Bihar caste seems to symbolize the identity of a person including the so-called educated persons. I would refer to my personal experience way back in 1971 when I was posted in Sahabad (now Arrah) Settlement. I was on tour to Buxar. I tried to find out the name of the Local Sub Divisional Officer (SDO) so that my wife and I could meet him in the evening. I enquired from the peon of the local office about the name of the SDO. The peon most candidly told me *Huzoor, SDO sahab ka nam maloom nahi par woh Gaya zila ka Brahmin ba* (Sir, I do not know the name of the SDO but he is a Brahmin from Gaya district). It is, however, a different matter though, during the election some Gram Panchayats, dominated by upper castes people, elected persons belonging to the Scheduled Castes or other extremely lower castes among the backward castes, as Mukhiya and, to start with, it is no mean achievement. This only shows that there is a realization that the virus of casteism needs to be checked.

The order of the Patna High Court dated March 19, 1996 refers to the fact that some of the Backward Castes in Bihar did not require reservation as they were otherwise politically strong. Therefore, I decided to collect the relevant information about the specific caste of the elected chairpersons of the Panchayats belonging to the Backward class of citizens. However, to my utter surprise I could not get this information which in the normal course the BDOs who are the Returning Officers should know. Nevertheless, I have collected information on the personal profile of only the elected chairpersons of Gram Panchayat, Panchayat Samiti and Zila Parishad on the above line which can be seen in Table 8.1, Table 8.2 and Table 8.3 respectively below:

Table 8.1: Personal Profile of Chairpersons (Mukhiya) of Gram Panchayat

		Number	*Percentage*
Age	21-30	887	11.52
	31-40	2679	34.48
	41-50	2240	28.84
	Above 50	1962	25.26
Educational Qualification	Literate	1712	22.08
	Matriculate	3382	43.62
	Graduate	2076	26.78
	Post Graduate	583	7.52
Gender	Male	7628	99.08
	Female	78	0.92
Caste	General	3084	40.95
	Backward	4264	56.63
	S.C.	143	1.90
	S.T.	39	0.52

Table 8.2: Personal Profile of Chairpersons (Pramukh) of Panchayat Samiti

		Number	*Percentage*
Age	21-30	95	18.93
	31-40	186	37.05
	41-50	106	21.11
	Above 50	115	22.91
Educational Qualification	Literate	53	10.56
	Matriculate	208	41.43
	Graduate	179	35.66
	Post Graduate	62	12.35
Gender	Male	475	89.28
	Female	54	10.72
Caste	General	171	33.93
	Backward	296	58.73
	S.C.	36	7.14
	S.T.	1	0.20

Table 8.3: Personal Profile of Chairpersons (Adhyaksha) of Zila Parishad

		Number	*Percentage*
Age	21-30	6	16.22
	31-40	16	43.24
	41-50	8	21.62
	Above 50	7	18.92
Educational Qualification	Literate	4	10.80
	Matriculate	13	35.14
	Graduate	13	35.14
	Post Graduate	7	18.92
Gender	Male	28	75.68
	Female	9	24.32
Caste	General	16	43.24
	Backward	21	56.75
	S.C.	0	0
	S.T.	0	0

The three Tables 8.1, 8.2 and 8.3 give us a very interesting picture about the personal profile of the elected chairpersons. If we look at the age profile of all the three categories of chairpersons, i.e., Mukhiya, Pramukh and Adhayaksha it will be seen that younger generation of the people are the dominant section in all the categories of the Panchayats. In fact, quite a sizeable number of them are below 30 years and a very high percentage of such elected chairpersons are within the age group of 40 years. The two most important posts as perceived by the people, i.e., Mukhiya of the Gram Panchayat and Adhayaksha of the Zila Parishad are dominated by the younger generation and only 25 per cent of the Mukhiyas and 19 per cent of the Adhayakshas are above 50.

Educational qualification-wise almost 80 per cent of the Mukhiyas are matriculate and above and about 27 per cent Mukhiyas are graduates with about 7 per cent as post graduate degree holders. Persons below matriculate accounts for about 10 per cent for the Pramukh and Adhayaksha while 22 per cent accounts for Mukhiya.

Gender-wise it has not been possible to achieve the required percentage in favour of women for the offices of chairpersons of the Panchayats for the reasons explained in the previous chapter.

As indicated earlier, it had not been possible to collect the required information about specific caste of the Backward Class of citizens even though the Commission has designed the proforma for getting such information also. Nevertheless, the three tables, i.e., Tables 8.1, 8.2 and 8.3 above, would reveal that more than 56 per cent of the chairpersons of the Panchayats at each of the three tiers belong to Backward Class of citizens. Thus, this section of the society has cornered the lion's share in the total offices of chairpersons of the Panchayats. The position is not likely to be any different in respect of members of the Panchayats. This is a reality in Bihar and if the Patna High Court has quashed Schedule-I of the Act and directed the State government to revise the list of Backward Class of citizens one should not get surprised.

At the beginning of Chapter 7 it has been brought out clearly that reservation is not an end in itself but a means to achieve certain end. If the end was to improve the social, economic and educational lot of the disadvantaged section of the population by transferring power to this section through the instrument of reservation it can be safely concluded that the purpose has been more than served in favour of the Backward Class of citizens without reservation. The crucial question will be whether this 56 per cent and more of the offices of chairpersons cornered by the Backward Class of citizens has been equitably shared by different castes that have been classified as Backward Class. In spite of its best effort the Commission could not collect specific backward caste-wise figures. However, very senior political leaders including some in the government belonging to the so-called Backward Castes have been quoted by various newspapers as claiming an impressive number of offices of chairpersons won by persons belonging to their castes. There is no reason to disbelieve such claim. The obvious conclusion would be that it is only the dominant castes among the Backward Class of citizens who have cornered these posts and their *inter se* number has been proportionate not so much to the numerical strength of a particular caste as to the political clout and muscle power of the caste concerned.

As against the impressive gains made by the Backward Class of citizens the achievement in favour of the Scheduled Castes, the Scheduled Tribes and women for the offices of Chairpersons of the Panchayat is very pathetic. This can be appreciated if we look at Table 7.4 and Table 7.5 in Chapter 7. If we make a comparison between the percentage achieved by the Backward Class of citizens and that achieved by the Scheduled Castes, the Scheduled Tribes and women for offices of chairpersons of the Panchayats it will be seen that as against more than 56 per cent achieved by the Backward Class of citizens the percentage has been very negligible in case of the Scheduled Castes, the Scheduled Tribes and the women. In fact, not a single post of Adhayaksha out of 37 posts has gone in favour of the Scheduled Castes or the Scheduled Tribes. The most dismal picture is in respect of Mukhiya who is the most important functionary in the whole system. As against 2,824 posts of Mukhiya admissible for women the achievement has been only 78. Persons belonging to the Scheduled Castes have won 143 posts of Mukhiya as against the minimum admissible number of 1,317 and for the Scheduled Tribes it is 39 as against minimum admissible number of 80.

9

The Signals and the Messages

We have seen in the previous chapters that election to the Panchayats, conducted after a gap of 23 years and under a completely new legal frame, has ushered in democratic decentralization of power at the grassroots level. There was widespread belief that there would be no election to the Panchayats in Bihar and that even if it could be held the State would witness large scale violence and bloodshed. All these apprehensions and so-called predictions were completely belied and the people in the rural areas proved beyond doubt, to the shocking surprise of the so-called political experts, that they might be illiterate but their wisdom should not be underestimated. It is no wonder that their elected representatives in the State Assembly and the Parliament had noted with shock and disbelief that they would be required to approach these very illiterate persons, whom many would have considered irrelevant, during elections to the State Assembly and the Parliament next time around. Therefore, the "little man" has made others aware of his presence in the political set-up of the State.

We have experienced how 50 years of Indian democracy has provided enough opportunity to so many leaders to come to limelight. However, the same elected representatives would raise a hue and cry when the democratic rights of self-governance guaranteed by the Constitution are to be transferred to the grassroots level. The argument is like democracy is safe "in my hand" but it is very dangerous if the same democratic right is given to "his" or "her" hand. During the Election process some elected responsible persons met me and told me that no doubt I may succeed in creating democratic institutions at the grassroots level but it would also mean spread of corruption in rural areas. When I told these persons that when a pauper, after getting elected as a people's representative, has amassed wealth in the form of house property or commercial property in urban area very few people will know about the wealth so acquired but when a Mukhiya of a Gram Panchayat or a member of a Panchayat shows even a small change in his life style with some semblance of opulence everybody in the rural areas would come to know about it and there would be a general talk about the sudden change in the lifestyle of their elected representatives. Of course, they were not apparently convinced with my argument that there would be an effective check on the elected representatives for fear of losing the election next time. These elected persons would have us believe that corruption is good in urban areas but not so good in rural areas while the reality is that these persons are panicky about their future without the support of the grassroots democrats.

There is a clear message that women power would dominate rural Bihar in due course and the last Panchayat election was only a beginning in that direction. About 45,000 women candidates have been elected as members of the three-tier Panchayat Institutions. In fact, every Panchayat will have at least one-third women members. One woman member is enough to silence the entire lot of male members as in the rural areas no male person would like to be publicly opposed by women. Already reports are there that woman members are playing an active role in the working of the Panchayats. One should not forget that women power is like flash flood. When such power comes out, it does so in unimaginable fury. So the interest of the society and the interest of the menfolk lie in gainful utilization of women power atleast for the health and education of the children which are basic requirements for the society. One can ignore the emerging women power at one's own peril.

There was also a fear that various extremist groups would indulge in large-scale violence in certain districts of Bihar. Election to the Panchayats demolished that theory. In fact, people ignored the boycott call given by the extremists and many of the known extremist persons contested election to the Panchayats and also got elected to various posts. Nowhere in Bihar election was cancelled due to any extremist activity. Therefore, transfer of power to the democratic institutions at the grassroots level would only encourage the various dissatisfied and extremist groups to join the main stream of the society and we should not ignore this aspect.

Some social scientists met me after visiting some districts when the election process was on. They told me that in the rural areas the *en bloc* voting by a particular caste in favour of a particular candidate belonging to the same caste would not work as the people of the same caste were questioning the merit of supporting the leaders of their caste who had so far used the poorer section of their caste as their tools without doing any positive work for the welfare of the community. In a place like Bihar, such a thinking itself in the rural areas is quite significant. The following two instances would throw some light on such silent changes that may eventually take place in rural Bihar.

A senior politician who had been cabinet minister in several governments for a very long time including the present regime, but out of favour at the moment, narrated two cases of a North Bihar district. In one Panchayat dominated by people belonging to so-called high castes with a lot of muscle power and landed property, the person elected as Mukhiya belongs to *mallah* (boatman) community. In another Panchayat, though the majority of the population belongs to Brahmin caste, the person elected as Mukhiya belongs to a Scheduled Caste. There are two types of explanation for such unusual outcome of the election to the two Gram Panchayats. One is that since the Mukhiya is elected by a simple majority, the votes secured by the elected Mukhiya were from a solid group belonging to the lower castes, while the upper castes votes got divided as there were too many contestants of the upper castes for the post. The other explanation, which looks more plausible, is that even people belonging to the so-called high castes were not happy with the arrogant behaviour of the candidates belonging to the same castes and, therefore, they voted for a candidate belonging to a lower caste who, in their perception, would be more sincere about his work and would give due respect to the opinion of all sections of the population. Besides these two cases, there were instances in which women in direct contest against male candidates, were elected as Mukhiya of many Gram Panchayats with people opting for women for their competence. In a State like Bihar with a rigid social system based on caste alignments such results are quite encouraging.

The frustrated younger generation, born after 1957, have taken over the leadership of not only the urban areas but also in the rural areas and the society and the government should not minimize the damage that this younger generation would do to the society if their hopes and aspirations are not taken care of. Almost 80 per cent of the elected representatives are below 50 years of age, a very significant development. Most of the sitting Mukhiyas lost the election and, therefore, the old method of controlling the society through the elder persons would no longer be acceptable.

The most significant message is that the "little man" and the women power cannot be taken for granted and his elected representatives have already started asserting their new found constitutional role in the democratic decentralization of self-governance. One story goes like this. After the election of the Chairman and the Vice Chairman of the Zila Parishads, the meeting of such constituted Zila Parishads was convened on different dates by different Zila Parishads. In one such meeting three ministers of the State government were present as ex-officio members of the Zila Parishad in their capacity as the local MLAs. These ex-officio members occupied the front seats in the meeting room. When the meeting started the chairman of the Zila Parishad, who was also presiding over the meeting, asked these three ex-officio members to vacate the front row seats for the elected members of the Zila Parishad with a request that the ex-officio members should occupy seats on the back rows. Though a bit discourteous it only proves the point that the elected representatives of the Panchayats should be given due prominence and they should be treated as the real representatives of the people at the grassroots level. This incident has created a sense of nervousness among MLAs, MLCs and MPs who are ex-officio members of the concerned Panchayat so much so that they make excuses for not attending the meeting of the Panchayats and instead send their representatives on pleas of preoccupation elsewhere. It is a different matter though that such requests for proxy members has not been accepted.

The voters in rural areas have given a clear message to the so-called well-informed educated section of the population that they have a mind of their own and they know when and how to make their mind known. They have judged each and every candidate on merit and expressed their opinion secretly on the ballot papers and the mind of the voters could be known only after the ballot boxes were opened. The voters came to the polling station as silently as they left in no time. Their silence was louder than the loud noises made by the media or self-opinionated persons about the outcome of the election.

No doubt the "little man" had the last laugh.

10

Election to the Municipalities

Introduction

With the enactment of the Constitution (74th) Amendment Act, 1992 effective from January 6, 1993 Part IX-A, the municipalities were made part of the Constitution. Accordingly, Article 243-P to Article 243-ZG were added to the Constitution. These amended (newly added) Articles in the Constitution provide for the constitution of municipalities, i.e., Nagar Panchayat (an area in transition from a rural area to an urban area), Municipal Council and Municipal Corporation and formation of wards for the purpose of conducting election to the municipalities. The amended Articles also provide for reservation of seats and offices of chairpersons of the municipalities in favour of the Scheduled Castes, the Scheduled Tribes and women. The Constitution also empowers the Legislature of the State to enact law to carry out the provisions of the Constitution. These Articles also provide the basis for conduct of election to the municipalities. As per the provisions of Article 243-ZA, the superintendence, direction and control of the preparation of electoral rolls for, and the conduct of, all elections to the municipalities shall be vested in the same State Election Commissioner appointed by the Governor under Article 243-K for the conduct of all elections to the Panchayats. Thus election to the Panchayats as well as the municipalities shall be conducted by the same State Election Commission.

No election to the municipalities took place after the 74th amendment to the Constitution referred to above. In fact, the last elections to the municipalities were held about two decades ago. We have seen in the preceding chapters that elections to the Panchayats were also held after 23 years. Thus the State of Bihar did not have any local self-government in the rural areas as also in the urban areas for more than two decades.

The procedure for the conduct of election to the municipalities is more or less similar to the procedure for the Panchayat polls. With the conduct of election to the Panchayats during April-May, 2001 the people in general and the urban people in particular became hopeful of the Urban Local Bodies (ULBs) coming into existence in near future. The State had functioning Urban Local Bodies, i.e., Municipal Corporation, Municipality and Notified Area Committee. Therefore, the democratic institutions of self-governance at the grassroots level in the urban areas are not an unknown concept to the people. But after the 74th Amendment of the Constitution, the Urban Local Bodies have acquired the constitutional status which empowers these Urban Local Bodies to undertake developmental activities in urban areas. Thus a qualitative change in the status of the Urban Local Bodies made all the difference in the interest that was noticed during election to the Municipalities conducted in April-June, 2002 after one year of election to the Panchayats during April-May, 2001.

There are five Municipal Corporations, 32 Nagar Parishads called Municipalities and 80 Nagar Panchayats earlier called Notified Area Committees. Basic data of the three categories of municipalities are indicated in Tables 10.1, 10.2 and 10.3 below:

Table 10.1: Municipal Corporation (Nagar Nigam)—Basic Data

Sl. No.	*Nagar Nigam*	*No. of Wards*
1.	Patna Nagar Nigam	57
2.	Gaya Nagar Nigam	40
3.	Bhagalpur Nagar Nigam	38
4.	Muzaffarpur Nagar Nigam	38
5.	Darbhanga Nagar Nigam	37
	Total	210

Table 10.2: Municipality (Nagar Parishad)—Basic Data

Sl. No.	Nagar Parishad	No. of Wards
1.	Barh Nagar Parishad	22
2.	Khagaul Nagar Parishad	22
3.	Danapur Nagar Parishad	28
4.	Mokamah Nagar Parishad	24
5.	Arrah Nagar Parishad	35
6.	Buxar Nagar Parishad	24
7.	Sasaram Nagar Parishad	30
8.	Dehri Dalmianagar Nagar Parishad	30
9.	Biharsharif Nagar Parishad	37
10.	Jehanabad Nagar Parishad	24
11.	Aurangabad Nagar Parishad	22
12.	Nawada Nagar Parishad	24
13.	Sitamarhi Nagar Parishad	22
14.	Hajipur Nagar Parishad	28
15.	Motihari Nagar Parishad	28
16.	Betiah Nagar Parishad	30
17.	Bagha Nagar Parishad	26
18.	Madhubani Nagar Parishad	24
19.	Samastipur Nagar Parishad	24
20.	Munger Nagar Parishad	35
21.	Jamalpur Nagar Parishad	28
22.	Lakhisarai Nagar Parishad	24
23.	Jamui Nagar Parishad	22
24.	Begusarai Nagar Parishad	26
25.	Chapra Nagar Parishad	34
26.	Siwan Nagar Parishad	28
27.	Saharsa Nagar Parishad	28
28.	Supaul Nagar Parishad	22
29.	Purnia Nagar Parishad	32
30.	Araria Nagar Parishad	22
31.	Kishanganj Nagar Parishad	26
32.	Katihar Nagar Parishad	35
	Total	866

Table 10.3: Municipality (Nagar Panchayat)—Basic Data

Sl. No.	Nagar Parishad	No. of Wards
1.	Fatuha Nagar Panchayat	18
2.	Masaurhi Nagar Panchayat	18
3.	Maner Nagar Panchayat	14
4.	Fulwarisharif Nagar Panchayat	20

(Contd.)

Table 10.3 *(Contd.)*

Sl. No.	*Nagar Parishad*	*No. of Wards*
5.	Bakhtiyarpur Nagar Panchayat	16
6.	Piro Nagar Panchayat	12
7.	Bihian Nagar Panchayat	12
8.	Jagdishpur Nagar Panchayat	14
9.	Dumraon Nagar Panchayat	18
10.	Bikramganj Nagar Panchayat	16
11.	Koath Nagar Panchayat	10
12.	Nokha Nagar Panchayat	12
13.	Nasriganj Nagar Panchayat	12
14.	Hilsa Nagar Panchayat	16
15.	Islampur Nagar Panchayat	14
16.	Silaw Nagar Panchayat	12
17.	Rajgir Nagar Panchayat	14
18.	Bhabhua Nagar Panchayat	16
19.	Bodh Gaya Nagar Panchayat	14
20.	Sherghati Nagar Panchayat	16
21.	Tekari Nagar Panchayat	10
22.	Makhdumpur Nagar Panchayat	14
23.	Rafiganj Nagar Panchayat	12
24.	Nawinagar Nagar Panchayat	10
25.	Daudnagar Nagar Panchayat	18
26.	Warsaliganj Nagar Panchayat	14
27.	Hisua Nagar Panchayat	12
28.	Nawgachhia Nagar Panchayat	18
29.	Sultanganj Nagar Panchayat	18
30.	Kahalgaon Nagar Panchayat	12
31.	Banka Nagar Panchayat	16
32.	Amarpur Nagar Panchayat	12
33.	Bargania Nagar Panchayat	16
34.	Belsand Nagar Panchayat	10
35.	Sheohar Nagar Panchayat	10
36.	Motipur Nagar Panchayat	12
37.	Kanti Nagar Panchayat	12
38.	Lalganj Nagar Panchayat	14
39.	Mahnar Nagar Panchayat	18
40.	Chakiya Nagar Panchayat	10
41.	Sugauli Nagar Panchayat	14
42.	Dhaka Nagar Panchayat	14
43.	Areraj Nagar Panchayat	10
44.	Raxaul Nagar Panchayat	16
45.	Chanpatia Nagar Panchayat	12
46.	Narkatiaganj Nagar Panchayat	18
47.	Ramnagar Nagar Panchayat	16

(*Contd.*)

Table 10.3 *(Contd.)*

Sl. No.	*Nagar Parishad*	*No. of Wards*
48.	Jaynagar Nagar Panchayat	12
49.	Jhanjharpur Nagar Panchayat	14
50.	Ghoghardiha Nagar Panchayat	10
51.	Dalsinghsarai Nagar Panchayat	12
52.	Rosra Nagar Panchayat	14
53.	Haweli Kharagpur Nagar Panchayat	16
54.	Barahiya Nagar Panchayat	18
55.	Jhajha Nagar Panchayat	18
56.	Shekhpura Nagar Panchayat	18
57.	Barbigha Nagar Panchayat	18
58.	Khagaria Nagar Panchayat	18
59.	Gogri Jamalpur Nagar Panchayat	14
60.	Sonepur Nagar Panchayat	16
61.	Dighwara Nagar Panchayat	14
62.	Madhora Nagar Panchayat	14
63.	Rivilganj Nagar Panchayat	16
64.	Maharajganj Nagar Panchayat	12
65.	Mairwa Nagar Panchayat	10
66.	Gopalganj Nagar Panchayat	20
67.	Mirganj Nagar Panchayat	12
68.	Barauli Nagar Panchayat	16
69.	Karaiya Nagar Panchayat	10
70.	Birpur Nagar Panchayat	10
71.	Nirmali Nagar Panchayat	10
72.	Madhepura Nagar Panchayat	18
73.	Murliganj Nagar Panchayat	14
74.	Kaswa Nagar Panchayat	14
75.	Banmankhi Nagar Panchayat	14
76.	Jogwani Nagar Panchayat	14
77.	Farwishganj Nagar Panchayat	18
78.	Bahadurganj Nagar Panchayat	14
79.	Thakurganj Nagar Panchayat	10
80.	Manihari Nagar Panchayat	12
	Total	1132

If we look at the number of the Urban Local Bodies and the number of wards for which commissioners/councillors are to be elected we realise that the problem in the conduct of election to the municipalities is most insignificant compared to the gigantic task of conducting election to a total number of 1,37,273 territorial constituencies (wards) of the three-tier Panchayat Institutions. Moreover, the Panchayat system is a three-tier one and every voter of a constituency would be required to exercise his right of franchise for four different posts simultaneously and, therefore, such a voter has a difficult task to judge the fitness of a candidate with reference to the responsibilities attached to a particular post. In the case of municipalities, there is no such tier system as every municipality, whether it is a Nagar Nigam or a Nagar Parishad or a Nagar Panchayat, is an independent legal entity and every candidate for a particular ward is judged by the voter with reference to not only the particular municipality but also the particular ward whose interest such a candidate is supposed to look after. Therefore, the task of a voter in election to the Urban Local Bodies is much simpler than that of a voter in an election to the Panchayats. Since the municipalities had no election for more than two decades the voters would be in a dilemma to select a candidate of their choice. As in the case of election to the Panchayats, large number of voters for election to the municipalities would also be exercising their right of franchise in such an election for the first time in about more than 40 years.

The Legal Frame

The Constitution (74th) Amendment Act, 1992 accorded constitutional status to the municipalities. In terms of Article 243-ZA the State Legislature enacted two Acts, the Bihar Municipal Act, 1922 (Bihar Act) and the Patna Municipal Corporation Act, 1951 (Patna Act) referred to earlier. Two Rules, namely, the Bihar Municipal Elections and Election Petitions Rules, 1953 (Bihar Rules) and the Patna Municipal Corporation Preparation of Electoral Rolls and Conduct of Election Rules, 1953 (Patna Rules) were framed by the government in terms of the relevant provisions of the two Acts referred to above. Though election to the municipalities had taken place in the past there were no separate Rules for constitution of territorial constituencies (wards) as mandated under the Constitution. The wards were earlier formed as per the executive instructions issued by the State government.

The State government have, however, framed two Rules, one for constituting wards of the municipalities and the other for constituting wards for the Municipal Corporations under the titles, the Bihar Municipalities Territorial Constituencies (Wards) Constitution Rules, 2001 and the Patna Municipal Corporation Territorial Constituencies (Wards) Constitution Rules, 2001. While the Patna Act and the relevant two sets of Rules referred to above would apply to all the five Municipal Corporations in the State, the Bihar Act and the relevant two sets of Rules would apply to all the municipalities other than the Municipal Corporations, i.e., all the Nagar Parishads and the Nagar Panchayats. Historically Patna Municipal Corporation came into existence earlier and hence the Patna Act was framed accordingly. The other four Municipal Corporations came into existence subsequently and the provisions of the Patna Act and the corresponding Rules were made applicable to these Municipal Corporations also in due course.

We have seen that the Act and the Rules relating to Panchayat elections are quite elaborate and comprehensive and whatever practical difficulties were faced during the course of election, the State government could amend the Rules immediately and there was no problem in conducting election to the Panchayats. However, in the case of Municipal Laws including the Rules the same are seriously flawed and there has not been any attempt by the State government to bring the two Acts and the two Rules in consonance with the provisions of the Constitution. The entire approach of the government has been very casual. If the government could find time to frame Act and Rules in respect of the Panchayats which are quite comprehensive, the reason for such lacklustre and casual approach of the government in respect of the Acts and the Rules relating to municipalities is beyond my comprehension. After the successful election to the Panchayats during April-May, 2001 the State government should have realized that there was no way by which the government could avoid election to the municipalities specially in view of the fact that the Patna High Court was regularly monitoring the matter while hearing the PIL pending before the Court. In fact, government should have utilized the benefits of the practical experience gathered during election to the Panchayats in making necessary amendments in both the Acts and the Rules relating to election to the municipalities.

There was indeed an attempt, though half-hearted, on the part of the government, to make amendments in the Bihar Rules and the Patna Rules relating to election to the municipalities. I did suggest some changes in the Rules based on my experience on the inadequacy of the Panchayat Rules and I appreciated the readiness of the government to accept the suggestions made by me by incorporating the same in the Rules which became quite effective in plugging the loopholes noticed in the Panchayat Rules. After the election was over I had suggested some amendments in the Panchayat Rules to the government and may be in due course those amendments could be incorporated. I could not make any suggestion on the Acts and the Rules relating to municipalities as I did not notice any interest in the concerned administrative department whereas the Department of Panchayati Raj took great initiative in utilizing the experiences gained by the Commission in amending the Rules. While the State government no doubt accepted most of my suggestions relating to amendments in the Bihar Rules and the Patna Rules relating to municipalities, certain avoidable obstacles, which were more amusing than real, continued. The two Rules referred to above do not have the required number of prescribed forms. Even the forms which are prescribed under the Rules need extensive modifications so that the same could be used to take care of any new situation. Since there was not enough time to devise new forms or revise the old forms I proposed to the government that there could be an omnibus provision in the two Acts or the two Rules enabling the Commission to devise new forms and/or to revise the existing forms as it deemed fit so that the Commission could not be handicapped during the process of election. I was told that the legal experts pointed out that it would not be proper to give such wide power to the Commission. I did not insist on the matter further as the thinking of the government was that the Commission which has the plenary power under the Constitution to take any action for the conduct of a free and fair election but a small power to devise a new form or to revise an existing form is more wide than the plenary power of the Commission. There was yet another amusing episode on my suggestion to make an enabling provision in the two Rules for the use of Electronic Voting Machine (EVM) during election to the municipalities. My idea was that at least in one ward of each of the five Municipal Corporations EVM could be used to educate the voters and the polling personnel and since the EVMs are supplied by the Election Commission of India it would not involve much expenditure. I was told that the highest authority at the official level was reluctant to give such wide power to the Commission. He was, however, prevailed upon and the enabling provisions were made in the Rules for use of EVMs. It was a different matter though I lost my interest as any reform in the system is an anathema in the State.

Since the State Election Commissioner has the plenary power under the Constitution I had no option but to issue elaborate and detailed guidelines on the conduct of election. I also revised the existing forms and also devised new ones, whenever necessary. In doing so I extensively utilized my experiences gained during election to the Panchayats. Since by now the Commission has established its credibility and independent identity among the people in general and the voters in particular, the guidelines issued by the Commission have been accepted by all concerned without any criticism. The fact that election to the municipalities was orderly and with least violence is a proof that the guidelines and instructions issued by the Commission had ensured a free and fair poll for the municipalities.

11

Conduct of Election to the Municipalities

Since the procedure for the conduct of electión to the Panchayats and election to the municipalities is more or less the same, I have utilized the experience gained during election to the Panchayats in preparing elaborate guidelines on every possible contingency. For record it would be useful to know that after the election was over all the instructions and guidelines issued by the Commission during election to the Panchayats and election to the municipalities were got printed in the form of compendia which have been forwarded to the field officers for use in future.

After the successful election to the Panchayats the district administration has become quite confident in conducting election to the Urban Local Bodies. By now the Commission has also proved its credibility and identity among the general public and they genuinely believed that the Commission would do everything possible to ensure a free and fair election. I consider this as a great asset for the Commission. The first two basic requirements for the conduct of election to the municipalities, or for that matter any election, are preparation of upto-date voters list and delimitation of constituencies (wards).

As regards the preparation of voters list the procedure is the same as prescribed for the preparation of voters list for election to the Panchayats. As in the case of Panchayats, the Patna Act and the Bihar Act provide that all such persons who are enrolled as electors in the electoral rolls or that part of the rolls of the State Legislative Assembly Constituency, for the time being in force, which is concerned with the territorial constituency of the Municipal Corporation/Nagar Parishad/Nagar Panchayat shall be the electors for the concerned Municipal Corporation/Nagar Parishad/Nagar Panchayat. While the voters list is prepared by the Election Commission of India booth-wise, the voters list for the Municipal election is to be prepared ward-wise and subsequently to be segregated booth-wise within the ward. Thus any mistake in distributing voters among concerned ward as also among the concerned booths within a ward would create a serious problem during the poll. The Rules provide for publication of draft electoral rolls inviting claims and objections and after disposal of claims and objections, if any, the final list is to be published. This was done as per the prescribed procedure. The Commission did not receive much complaint on this account.

The real problem faced by the election machinery was the constitution of wards. As per the provisions of the Constitution and the Acts, a Municipality is to be divided into territorial constituencies called wards and one Commissioner/Councillor is to be elected for every ward directly by the voters of every such ward. In the past wards were constituted as per executive instructions issued by the Government. As indicated earlier, government has framed two different Rules, one for the Municipal Corporations and the other for the municipalities (Nagar Parishad and Nagar Panchayat) for constituting wards. Thus it was altogether a new exercise for the District Magistrates who were also the District Election Officers none of whom would perhaps have any past experience for constituting wards of the municipalities election to which was to be held after two decades. The basic data about the municipalities at a glance can be seen at Table 11.1 below:

Table 11.1: Basic Data of Municipalities

Sl. No.	*Type of Municipalities*	*Number of Municipalities*	*Number of wards*	*Number of voters*
1.	Municipal Corporation	5	210	1670338
2.	Nagar Parishad	32	866	2106391
3.	Nagar Panchayat	80	1132	1321472
	Total	117	2208	5098209

While the Rules prescribe population as the yardstick for constituting the number of wards of a particular municipality, it was a difficult task for the field officers to arrive at the correct figure of population of a municipality. As per the law the population figure of 1991 census should be the basis whereas before election to the municipalities was to be held, the provisional figure of population of 2001 census was already available. There is no denying the fact that there has been substantial increase in population over the last one decade. For various reasons there has been steady flow of people from the rural areas to the urban areas and such people who have migrated to the urban areas have settled only in certain localities in the urban areas depending on their vocation or social factors. In other words, such settlements of the migrants in the urban areas have not been evenly distributed. In the case of Patna Municipal Corporation area there has been an increase of 50 per cent in the population during last one decade. It became a difficult task for the Commission to carve out the boundary of wards and also simultaneously reconcile the population figure taking into account the legally admissible population figure as per 1991 census and the actual population in position based on 2001 census.

While constituting the wards the Commission had to evolve a practical way out so that provisions of the Rules relating to constitution of wards would be complied with to the extent feasible. The Rules provide that the number of population of every ward within the municipality should be same to the extent practicable. I, therefore, worked out a standard population for a ward with a variation of ±500 for a municipality with a population upto 1,50,000 and with a variation of ±1000 for a municipality with a population exceeding 1,50,000. If in the process it was found that even after allowing for ±500 or ±1000, as stated above, it would not be possible to work out the standard figure of population in any ward, specific approval of the Commission was to be taken.

The most difficult problem faced in constituting wards was in the transfer of certain number of households to a particular ward so as to comply with the provisions of the Rules. In such a case the practical problem was that if certain number of households, say 20, were to be transferred to a particular ward to get the standard figure of population, it might not be necessary that these 20 households to be transferred would have separate line of demarcation by natural or artificial objects like road, street or any landmark building etc. In such cases where practical difficulties were faced the Commission had given specific approval.

The Commission did not receive much complaint about formation of ward and ward-wise preparation of voters list. Whatever complaints were received were disposed of promptly. However, when the election process started it was noticed that in some cases, specially in the case of Patna Municipal Corporation, there were serious irregularities in the preparation of voters list and at least in eight wards the voters residing in a particular ward were shown as enrolled in the voters list of another ward. Whether it happened on account of any genuine omission on the part of the officers involved in the work or it was done deliberately to benefit certain candidates is difficult to say. But the irregularities were so serious that the Commission had to cancel election to these eight wards of Patna Municipal Corporation just two days before the scheduled date of poll. The Commission also debarred the concerned officers from election related work. This was given wide publicity by the print media and it created a very strong deterrent on potentially delinquent officers with the result that the election to the municipalities was not only free and fair but was almost violence free. The voters list of eight wards of the Patna Municipal Corporation was rectified in due course and election to these wards were conducted separately at a later date.

While constituting the wards the Commission was surprised to see that in most of the cases there was no existing map of the municipalities showing the geographical boundary of the concerned municipality much less the boundaries of the wards of the municipality concerned. The Rules do not provide for preparation of map of a municipality. The time at the disposal of the Commission was also short and I could not force the District Election Officers to prepare maps to the scale. However, on my instruction the District Election Officers got the maps prepared ward-wise though the same were not always to the scale. But definitely this would be a draft map for preparing a proper map to the scale before the next election.

The same district administration involved in conducting election to the Panchayats is also the election machinery for election to the municipalities within the district concerned. Filing of nomination and scrutiny thereof were smooth and by and large there was no serious complaint against the Returning Officers. Nevertheless, the Commission faced certain new situation not originally envisaged.

When issuing instructions on filing nomination the Commission anticipated that some eunuchs commonly known as *hizra* could be candidates in election to the municipalities. The Commission clarified the matter thus. An eunuch candidate would contest election from any of the unreserved wards. If, however, such a candidate claims to be a member of the Scheduled Castes or the Scheduled Tribes a caste certificate to that effect issued by a competent officer would be required for filing nomination for a ward reserved for the Scheduled Castes or the Scheduled Tribes, as the case may be. An eunuch candidate was debarred from contesting election from a ward reserved for women. The rationale behind such decision was that the Commission went by the accepted definition of "female" as being a person biologically capable of or having the biological potentiality of giving birth to young one. Since eunuch does not have such biological potentiality or capability the Commission could not declare an eunuch as female. However, during the election to the Patna Municipal Corporation a eunuch candidate filed nomination for a ward reserved for women and in support of the claim the candidate produced certain documents about sex. The matter was brought to the notice of the Commission which was in a fix and a decision was to be given immediately. I considered the matter in great detail and came to the conclusion that the sex of such a candidate should be decided on the basis of the entry made in the concerned Municipal electoral roll and if there is a difference between the entry in the electoral roll for Municipal Corporation and the corresponding entry in the electoral roll of the Election Commission of India for State Legislative Assembly the latter entry would prevail. Accordingly, necessary clarification was issued to the District Election Officer, Patna. To the great relief of the Commission and the District Election Officer, Patna, it was found that the particular eunuch candidate had a photo identity card issued by the Election Commission of India and the relevant entry in the photo identity card and that in the electoral roll prepared by the Election Commission of India has shown the concerned eunuch as female. Thus "she" contested election from a ward reserved for women and got also elected.

The above decision of the Commission was flashed on the TV by a National channel with wide coverage continuously throughout the day highlighting that Bihar State Election Commission has declared a eunuch as female. Even in a tense situation I could not help most gleefully enjoying the humour and my newly discovered expertise in determining the gender of a person.

Compared to about 180 million ballot papers to be printed for election to the Panchayats the estimated number of ballot papers for election to the municipalities was within six millions. I thought the two State Government Presses could be in a position to print such small number of ballot papers. But this was not to be. While one Printing Press expressed its inability to print the ballot papers due to lack of required resources, the other Printing Press conveyed its willingness to do the job subject to the condition that the ballot paper should be printed in phases over one month subject to supply of electricity, besides all other facilities and finally, it was conveyed that no paper was available for printing the ballot papers. The Commission, therefore, had no option but to get the ballot papers printed by the same Printing Press of a neighbouring State Government Undertaking which had printed the ballot papers for Panchayat election. The Commission devised and approved the form and design of the ballot paper, a specimen of which can be seen at Appendix-B.

We have seen that during election to the Panchayats some Returning Officers misled the candidates about acceptance of nomination. To obviate such contingencies in election to the municipalities it was made mandatory for the Returning Officer to inform a candidate, whose nomination was found valid after scrutiny and withdrawal, in writing, in a format prescribed by the Commission that his/her nomination has been accepted and that a particular election symbol, the specimen of which is to be printed on the letter itself, has been allotted to him or her. Thus a validly nominated candidate for election to the Municipalities had a written confirmation from the Returning Officer about the acceptance of nomination and allotment of a particular symbol. This decision of the Commission was welcomed by each and every candidate.

Election was held as per schedule on April 28, 2002 except that election to the Patna Municipal Corporation was held on April 30, 2002 and election to the eight wards of Patna Municipal Corporation, which was cancelled due to irregularities and election to the two new municipalities and few wards where election was countermanded, were held on June 16, 2002.

Counting of votes was completed as per schedule. To make sure that a Returning Officer would not commit any mistake in declaring result after counting it was made obligatory for the Returning Officer to sign the final result sheet and for an Observer deputed by the Commission to countersign. Only then could the result be announced and thereafter election certificate issued to the winning candidates. This instruction of the Commission eliminated the last cause of any complaint by the contesting candidates. It will be relevant to mention here that the Rules do not have any prescribed format for issuing election certificate. I, therefore, devised the certificate on the same line as is used by a University for awarding Degree to a successful student for issuing election certificate to the winning candidates.

With the declaration of results and issue of certificates to the winning candidates the election process started in February, 2001 for ushering in democratic decentralization of self-governance in the rural and urban came to an end.

Before the election process for the Urban Local Bodies started apprehensions were expressed and highlighted by the print media that there would be large scale violence in the urban areas where the people would be vocal and would always remain alert. Rigging or booth capturing was also apprehended. In other words, conduct of a free and fair election was very much in doubt. Let us see whether such apprehensions were justified or not.

Compared to the high voting percentage in election to the Panchayats, the voting percentage in election to the Urban Local Bodies was comparatively low between 55 and 60 while in certain areas the percentage exceeded this. However, the enthusiasm shown by women candidates and voters was unprecedented and election to both Panchayats and Urban Local Bodies witnessed identical response by women in general.

There was no complaint about rigging or booth capturing in the election to the Urban Local Bodies. The voters were free and they came in large numbers to cast their votes and the entire election process passed off in an orderly manner. The voters had by then developed enough confidence in the election machinery in ensuring a free and fair election.

I have tried to probe into such an unusual happening as to how there was no serious attempt by any candidate or his supporters to do rigging or booth capturing. It transpired that the contesting candidates were keen that election would take place to enable them to enjoy the benefit of local self-governance. But the most deterrent factor was my decision to allot "zero" number of votes in a polling station where rigging or booth capturing has taken place during election to the Panchayats dealt with in Chapter 5 earlier. I had taken the plea that no rigging or booth capturing could take place without the direct or indirect support of the candidates or their supporters, including the polling agents and, therefore, the contesting candidates should be made to suffer for any act of rigging or booth capturing in a particular polling station. The Commission made it clear that if rigging takes place in a polling station the contesting candidates would be held responsible. This resulted in a very effective check on miscreants.

Another factor that put a check on persons with criminal antecedent filing nomination for election to the Urban Local Bodies was the declaration to be signed by the candidate and two witnesses along with details of pending cases against such a candidate in a prescribed form at Appendices D and E. This has been dealt with in Chapter 6, hence I am not going into further details here. The signature of two witnesses with their full names and addresses in the declaration made all the difference with the result that there was no report of any candidate with criminal background filing nomination or being elected as Ward Commissioner/Councillor of any municipality.

On the question of whether election to the Urban Local Bodies was free or not we will see that there was a qualitative change in the incidents of violence during election to the Urban Local Bodies. In the entire State only three unfortunate incidents took place with three precious lives lost in Gaya Municipal Corporation area. Of these three, one young man lost his life when the hand bomb carried by him exploded killing him on the spot. Incidentally, this young man was trying to ensure victory of his mother who was a candidate. I do not know whether the mother won or not but she definitely did lose her son for ever. The other two incidents, also in

Gaya Municipal Corporation area, related to killings of two anti-social elements while they were trying to capture booths. They were shot dead by the security personnel on duty. These two unfortunate incidents would only prove that the security personnel did their job in a commendable manner though unfortunately the two anti-social elements had to lose their lives.

There was some commotion in about four to five pockets in Patna Municipal Corporation area when police had to open fire to disperse some unruly crowd. One could imagine the provocation in such cases. But everybody was surprised that there was no reaction against such police firing. There was no injury also due to police firing.

From what has been stated hereinbefore it would not be unreasonable to conclude that election to the Urban Local Bodies was free and fair and it was almost violence free. The three unfortunate incidents that happened in Gaya Municipal Corporation area could not be helped as otherwise the three miscreants who lost their lives would have created a serious law and order problem during the election.

12

Personal Profile of the Elected Commissioner/Councillor of the Municipalities

As indicated earlier, it has not been possible for me to prescribe a format in advance for collecting certain relevant data that go into the personal profile of a ward member or chairperson of a Panchayat. Subsequently, I collected the relevant information about the chairpersons only of the Panchayats which has been dealt with in Chapter 8 earlier.

Learning by the experience of the inadequacy in this respect during election to the Panchayats, I devised necessary formats for collecting certain relevant data about the candidates contesting election to the municipalities by making it mandatory to furnish such information along with nomination. As in the case of Panchayats, in the case of municipalities also I could not get the specific caste of the winning candidates belonging to Backward Class of citizens. Nevertheless, it has been possible for the Commission to collect the relevant data of age, educational qualification, gender, caste and three additional items on marital status, profession and annual income of the winning Ward Commissioner/ Councillor.

The personal profile of elected Commissioners/ Councillors of Municipal Corporation, Nagar Parishad and Nagar Panchayat can be seen respectively in the following three tables, *i.e.*, Table 12.1, Table 12.2 and Table 12.3:

Table 12.1: Personal Profile of Elected Councillors of Municipal Corporation

		Number	*Percentage*
Age (in Yrs.)	21-30	59	28.92
	31-40	70	34.31
	41-50	53	25.98
	Above 50	22	10.79
Educational Qualification	Literate	77	37.56
	Matriculate	50	24.40
	Graduate	46	24.43
	Post Graduate	32	15.61
Gender	Male	134	65.05
	Female	72	34.95
Marital Status	Married	187	91.22
	Unmarried	18	8.78
Caste	General	81	39.32
	Backward	107	51.94
	S.C.	18	8.74
	S.T.	0	0
Profession	Business	80	38.83
	Others	126	61.17
Annual Income (in Rs.)	≤ 50,000	181	87.02
	> 50,000	19	9.13
	> 1,00,000	08	3.85

Table 12.2: Personal Profile of Elected Commissioners of Nagar Parishad

		Number	*Percentage*
Age (in Yrs.)	21-30	254	30.13
	31-40	329	39.02
	41-50	170	20.17
	Above 50	90	10.68
Educational Qualification	Literate	357	41.56
	Matriculate	257	29.92
	Graduate	184	21.42
	Post Graduate	61	7.10
Gender	Male	561	65.16
	Female	300	34.84
Marital Status	Married	775	90.01
	Unmarried	86	9.99

(Contd.)

Table 12.2 (*Contd.*)

		Number	*Percentage*
Caste	General	293	34.35
	Backward	453	53.11
	S.C.	106	12.43
	S.T.	1	0.11
Profession	Business	263	30.55
	Others	598	69.45
Annual Income (in Rs.)	≤ 50,000	750	88.55
	> 50,000	74	8.73
	> 1,00,000	23	2.72

Table 12.3: Personal Profile of Elected Commissioners of Nagar Panchayat

		Number	*Percentage*
Age (in Yrs.)	21-30	333	30.55
	31-40	398	36.51
	41-50	250	22.94
	Above 50	109	10.00
Educational Qualification	Literate	520	47.02
	Matriculate	364	32.92
	Graduate	166	15.00
	Post Graduate	56	5.06
Gender	Male	707	63.12
	Female	413	36.88
Marital Status	Married	1050	93.92
	Unmarried	68	6.08
Caste	General	336	30.08
	Backward	596	53.36
	S.C.	183	16.38
	S.T.	2	0.18
Profession	Business	271	24.39
	Others	840	75.61
Annual Income (in Rs.)	≤ 50,000	1036	93.50
	> 50,000	60	5.42
	> 1,00,000	12	1.08

If we look at the age profile in the above three tables we will notice that most of the Ward Commissioners/Councillors are within the age group of 50 and only about 10 per cent of these elected representatives are above the age group of 50.

This is uniformly same in all the three categories of municipalities, i.e., Municipal Corporation, Nagar Parishad and Nagar Panchayat. There is a distinct similarity in the age profile of the elected representatives of the Panchayats and the elected representatives of the municipalities. The younger generation has higher representation in the municipalities and about 30 per cent of the ward members are within the age of 30 years in all the three categories of municipalities. In fact, about 70 per cent of the ward members are within 40 years of age. As the election took place after almost two decades a large number of candidates as also the voters took part in election to the municipalities for the first time in their life in more than 40 years.

Educational qualification-wise the scenario is a bit disappointing as urban areas were expected to send more educated ward members. But this has not happened. In fact, the number of post graduate degree holders elected as ward members was about 15 per cent for the Municipal Corporation, seven per cent for Nagar Parishad and only five per cent for Nagar Panchayat. The graduate degree holders account for more than 24 per cent in the Municipal Corporation while more than 21 per cent of the Nagar Parishad ward members are degree holders with still a lower figure of 15 per cent for Nagar Panchayat. Another shocking disclosure is that the Municipal Corporations which are supposed to provide better facility for education account for more than 37 per cent of the Ward Councillors who are only literate which no doubt is a very sad reflection on the spread of education in the five Municipal Corporations that include the one at the State capital.

Sex-wise representation and caste-wise representation (the Scheduled Castes and the Scheduled Tribes only) have been as per the provisions of the two Acts. However, caste-wise (other than the reserved castes) representation as ward members of the municipalities has been more or less on the same line as noticed in respect of the chairpersons of the three-tier Panchayat Institutions. The backward castes account for almost a uniform 53 per cent of the ward members in all the three categories of municipalities with 52 per cent for the Municipal Corporations, 53 per cent for Nagar Parishads and over 53 per cent for Nagar Panchayats. Representation of the Scheduled Castes and for women has been as per the provisions of the two Acts and there has not been any shortfall on this account. After the division of Bihar, the Scheduled Tribes population in urban areas got reduced drastically and, therefore, only two Ward Commissioners were elected for Nagar Panchayat and one Ward Commissioner for Nagar Parishad without any representation for the Scheduled Tribes in any of the five Municipal Corporations compared to higher number of posts going in favour of the Scheduled Tribes in the Panchayats. Going by the public claims made by various responsible persons and highlighted by the print media, it was clear that lion's share of ward members of the municipalities has been cornered by the predominant castes among the Backward Class of citizens.

Unmarried Ward Commissioners account for 6 per cent in the Nagar Panchayats with 9 per cent in Municipal Corporations and with slightly higher percentage of 10 in the Nagar Parishads. This again proves that people marry still at a very lower age as very few of the Ward Commissioners between the age group of 21-30 are not married.

If we look at the profession-wise percentage of the ward members it will be seen that quite a sizeable number of elected ward members is engaged in business as a profession with about 39 per cent for Municipal Corporations, 30.55 per cent for Nagar Parishads and 24.39 per cent for Nagar Panchayats. The expression "business" would include manufacturing activities and simple trading also though in the context of the State "business" mostly comprises trading activities.

Income-wise also a small number of ward members would have an annual income of more than Rs. 100,000 with majority of the members with annual income not exceeding Rs. 50,000 and this only proves that people in lower income group has been elected in large numbers.

The Commission has also collected relevant data on the personal profile of chairpersons of the Municipalities. The following three tables, i.e., Table 12.4, Table 12.5 and Table 12.6 would give the personal profile of the elected chairpersons of Municipal Corporations, Nagar Parishads and Nagar Panchayats respectively:

Table 12.4: Personal Profile of Chairpersons of Municipal Corporation

		Number	*Percentage*
Age (in Yrs.)	21-30	1	20.00
	31-40	2	40.00
	41-50	2	40.00
	Above 50	0	0.00
Educational Qualification	Literate	1	20.00
	Matriculate	1	20.00
	Graduate	3	60.00
	Post Graduate	0	0.00
Gender	Male	3	60.00
	Female	2	40.00
Marital Status	Married	5	100.00
	Unmarried	0	0.00
Caste	General	1	20.00
	Backward	3	60.00
	S.C.	1	20.00
	S.T.	0	0.00
Profession	Business	3	60.00
	Others	2	40.00
Annual Income (in Rs.)	≤ 50,000	4	80.00
	> 50,000	0	0.00
	> 1,00,000	1	20.00

Table 12.5: Personal Profile of Chairpersons of Nagar Parishad

		Number	*Percentage*
Age (in Yrs.)	21-30	7	21.88
	31-40	10	31.25
	41-50	11	34.37
	Above 50	4	12.50
Educational Qualification	Literate	10	31.25
	Matriculate	13	40.62
	Graduate	6	18.75
	Post Graduate	3	9.38
Gender	Male	18	56.25
	Female	14	43.75

(Contd.)

Table 12.5 (*Contd.*)

		Number	*Percentage*
Marital Status	Married	31	96.87
	Unmarried	1	3.13
Caste	General	14	43.75
	Backward	12	37.50
	S.C.	6	18.75
	S.T.	0	0
Profession	Business	11	34.37
	Others	21	65.63
Annual Income	≤ 50,000	27	84.37
(in Rs.)	> 50,000	2	6.26
	> 1,00,000	3	9.37

Table 12.6: Personal Profile of Chairpersons of Nagar Panchayat

		Number	*Percentage*
Age (in Yrs.)	21-30	17	21.52
	31-40	27	34.18
	41-50	23	19.11
	Above 50	12	15.19
Educational	Literate	37	46.84
Qualification	Matriculate	26	32.91
	Graduate	12	15.19
	Post Graduate	4	5.06
Gender	Male	45	56.96
	Female	34	43.04
Marital Status	Married	76	96.20
	Unmarried	3	3.80
Caste	General	26	32.91
	Backward	41	51.90
	S.C.	12	15.19
	S.T.	0	0
Profession	Business	29	36.71
	Others	50	63.29
Annual Income	≤ 50,000	69	87.34
(in Rs.)	> 50,000	7	8.86
	> 1,00,000	3	3.80

If we look at the age profile of the chairpersons it will be seen that younger generation is dominant in all the three categories of municipalities. In fact, the Mayors of all the five Municipal Corporations are within the age group of 50 with one Mayor within the age of 30 years and none is above 50 years of age. Same is the case in respect of Nagar Parishads where only about 12 per cent of the chairpersons are above the age group of 50. In case of Nagar Panchayats the age profile shows that about 15 per cent of the chairpersons is above the age of 50.

Educational qualification-wise none of the five Mayors of the Corporations is a post graduate degree holder while more than nine per cent of the Chairpersons and five per cent of the Chairpersons of Nagar Parishads and Nagar Panchayats respectively are post graduate degree holders. One of the Mayors is only a literate while the percentage of literate Chairpersons is 31.25 per cent for Nagar Parishads and as high as 46.84 per cent for Nagar Panchayats.

Sex-wise and caste-wise (the Scheduled Castes and the Scheduled Tribes only) representations have been as per the provisions of the two Acts.

The backward castes are predominant in respect of the Chairpersons of Municipal Corporation and Nagar Panchayat. 60 per cent of the Chairpersons of the Municipal Corporations and 52 per cent of the Chairpersons of the Nagar Panchayats have been cornered by the backward class of citizens. It is only in respect of Chairpersons of Nagar Parishads that the percentage of backward caste Chairpersons is about 37 and 44 per cent posts have gone in favour of the general category of persons. Here again going by the public pronouncements by responsible persons it appears that the dominant castes among the Backward Class of citizens have cornered the lion's share of Chairpersons in all the three categories of Municipalities.

Profession-wise business accounts for 60 per cent of the posts of Chairpersons for Municipal Corporation while about 34 per cent and 37 per cent account for the Nagar Parishad and the Nagar Panchayat respectively. Thus in respect of Chairpersons of Nagar Parishad and Nagar Panchayat representation from the business class has been quite low.

Annual income-wise only 20 per cent, 9.37 per cent and 3.80 per cent account for the Chairpersons of the Municipal Corporations, Nagar Parishads and Nagar Panchayats respectively with annual income of more than Rs. 100,000. Majority of the Chairpersons are with annual income equivalent or less than Rs. 50,000.

13

Some Fodder for Amusement

Going by the overall response of the district administration in conducting election to the Panchayats, in retrospect, I feel that the field officers involved in the election related work did a commendable job and they might have been under tremendous physical and mental stress for more than three months. But as a source of relaxation for the Commission, which was otherwise in a very tense mental frame, I briefly record few amusing episodes.

As we have seen earlier that in large number of cases election was to be cancelled due to printing error in the ballot papers. A very unusual mistake was about the surname of a particular candidate who himself did not notice the error while casting his vote and realized it only when a co-voter jokingly remarked "*Chaubeyjee polling booth se Singhjee ho kar nikal aye* (Chaubeyjee comes out of the polling booth as Singhjee). When the Commission pulled up the District Magistrate his answer was that it was a "clerical error" which even an illiterate man would not commit in the district where the prevalent caste structure would not allow anybody to declare a Chaubeyjee (a Brahmin) as Singhjee (usually a Rajput).

Immediately after election to the Panchayats was over there were some unfortunate incidents in which a few elected Mukhiyas were killed due to personal rivalry. Immediately, the vested interest opposed to the very idea of transferring power to the Panchayats, their public posture to the contrary notwithstanding, started a malicious canard that these

Mukhiyas would not have been killed but for the election to the Panchayats. It was a completely fallacious argument that "after it, therefore, due to it" which in logic is known as *post hoc, ergo propter hoc.* It is nothing but confusing consequence with sequence. Vested interests were trying seriously to convince the government that some way be found to remove the Mukhiyas (read inconvenient Mukhiyas) by a resolution expressing want of confidence in them by a majority of not less than two-thirds of the total number of voters of the Gram Panchayat in a special meeting under sub-section (4) of section 18 of the Act. The sub-section also provides that no such motion of no confidence shall be moved against any Mukhiya or Upmukhiya during the first two years of their tenure. Since a period of two years was considered by the vested interest too long a very malicious suggestion was doing the rounds that the requirement of two years be reduced to one year and the requirement of not less than two-thirds of the total number of voters be reduced to not less than one-tenths of the total number of voters and accordingly amendment be made in sub-section (4). Some saner elements opposed the idea on grounds that it would amount to circumvention of the constitutional mandate but such elements were shouted down. However, apparently good sense prevailed and, may be due to the fear of the Patna High Court coming in the way of such a draconian attempt, the elected Panchayat bodies have been allowed to survive so far.

The feudal elements were dead against reservation for the offices of Chairpersons of municipalities. In one case the majority members refused to elect the Chairperson of a municipality simply because the post of Chairperson for the particular municipality has been reserved for a Scheduled Caste Ward Commissioner. An attempt was made to first elect the Vice-Chairman of their choice so that the functioning of the municipality could be carried on without the Chairman. Since the post of Vice-Chairman is not reserved, the majority members could find it very easy to run the municipality with the Vice-Chairman taking advantage of the provisions of the Act that the Vice-Chairman can run the affairs of the municipality in the absence of the Chairman. The Commission got some hints about such possibility in other municipalities also and accordingly I made it mandatory that the election of Vice-Chairman of a municipality shall take place only after the election of the Chairperson. This effectively sealed the evil design of these vested interests.

In another case some elected members belonging to the general category of persons met me and complained that they had no idea before the election that the office of Chairperson of their municipality would be reserved as otherwise they would have put up a candidate from the reserved category of their choice. Since in this case the person to be elected as Chairperson on the reserved post was not a man of their choice they felt frustrated. Apparently these people were not opposed to reservation for the office of the Chairperson of the municipality as such but grudged their inability to get a "yes man" elected to the post.

14

Conclusion

One can conclude that elections to the PRIs and ULBs in Bihar were reasonably free and fair and the scale of violence was not as projected by the so-called well-informed but self-opinionated persons. It also proves that the political leadership is totally detached from the ground reality and the cynical contempt entertained by the so-called people's representatives for the voters at the grassroots level has been replaced by a sense of panic and nervousness in the State leadership after the successful elections to the PRIs/ULBs.

50 years of democracy in the country made the poor and the illiterate, but not unintelligent, villagers aware of their democratic rights under the Constitution to decide for themselves what is good for them. Once given the opportunity such simple rural people can make their presence felt and they have demonstrated that in ample manner through ballots.

The rural people did not require any canvassing that is commonly witnessed during election to the Parliament and the State Assemblies. Denial of democratic right of local self-governance for more than two decades has resulted in widespread dissatisfaction in the minds of the rural people and no government in future can ignore the hopes and aspirations of the common people.

Playing caste card by the vested interests for remaining in power did not succeed in elections to the PRIs. In many cases, merits of a candidate rather than his/her caste or creed or sex has decided the result of the elections. In rural Bihar, caste is a dominant factor, but election to the PRIs held in April, 2001 has proved that casteism would not pay in future.

Women in general remain the most oppressed lot in the society specially in rural areas irrespective of their socio-economic status. Though there is no reservation for the post of Chairperson in favour of women, many women candidates got elected as Mukhiya of Gram Panchayats against male candidates. Their new found role as Members of the PRIs under the Constitution has made a sea change in the rural Bihar as women voters came out in large numbers freely on the day of poll and women power is going to make a significant impact on the socio-economic life of the rural people.

A significant outcome of elections to the PRIs is that vested interest will not succeed in their attempt to derail the democratic process in future and the State level and national level political leadership has already started realising their reduced relevance in the rural areas where the writ of the Mukhiyas alone prevails.

Another significant development has been the emergence of the youths in the democratic institutions of self-governance at the grassroots level both in the rural areas and in urban areas. In fact, the younger generation specially those born after 1957 has participated in the elections to the PRIs and ULBs for the first time in their life and this generation has been the predominant group among the elected members and Chairpersons of these institutions. Any attempt by the political leadership at the State level or at the national level to ignore this dominant group would create social unrest.

Elected members of the PRIs and the ULBs are fully conscious of their democratic rights under the Constitution and they have already started asserting their new found status and power.

That the intervening period between 1978 when election to the PRIs was last held and 2001 when elections to the PRIs held in accordance with the amended provisions of the Constitution is an aberration has been fully established. The democratic aspirations of the people cannot be suppressed for long.

As in the case of election to the PRIs, election to the ULBs has also established the fact that common people are law abiding and if the election machinery is impartial in the conduct of election, any attempt by the miscreants and anti-social elements to disturb the democratic process would be foiled by the voters themselves and they have proved that in ample manner during elections to the PRIs and elections to the ULBs.

Appendix-A

Specimen of Ballot Paper (Panchayat)

BIHAR PANCHAYAT ELECTION, 2001

MEMBER OF GRAM PANCHAYAT

District - / Block - / Gram Panchayat - Territorial Constituency No. -

Voter's Serial No. -

GPS - 1/0001

Voter's Signature / Thumb Impression

Member of Gram Panchayat/ Distt. - / Block -

Mahendra Prasad Narayan Sinha

Gram Panchayat / Territorial Constituency No. -

Shyam Nandan Prasad Narayan

GPS - 1/0001

Ram Chandra Singh

Bhupendra Singh

Ram Nagina Rai

Appendix-B

Specimen of Ballot Paper (Municipality)

NAGAR NIGAM ELECTION, 2002

WARD COUNCILLOR OF NAGAR NIGAM

Patna Municipal Corporation/ Ward No.

Voter's Serial No. –

PMC–1/000001

Voter's Signature / Thumb Impression

Patna Municipal Corporation/ Ward No. -

Sunil Kumar Srivastava

Rajiv Shankar

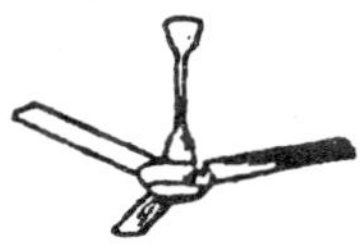

PMC - 1/000001

Sanjay Kumar

Sumitav Aroon

Xavier Lawrence Sah

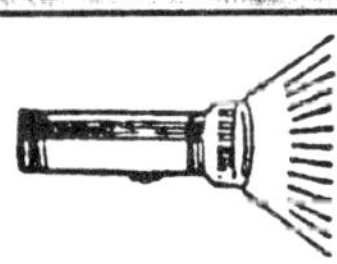

Appendix-C

Form of Affidavit (Panchayat)

I, ... , S/o/D/o /W/o .... aged .... years, a resident of Village .... Police Station .... District ...., hereby declare on oath:

that I am filing the nomination paper for election to the post of Mukhiya of Gram Panchayat ..../Member of Gram Panchayat/Panchayat Samiti/Zila Parishad ....;

that I am fully conversant with the provisions of Section 139 of the Bihar Panchayat Raj Act, 1993, as amended;

that I am not ineligible for election or for holding the post after election as the Mukhiya/Member of Gram Panchayat, Member of Panchayat Samiti and Member of Zila Parishad under section 139 of the Bihar Panchayat Raj, 1993 as amended.

Signature of the Deponent.

Place :

Date :

Note: To be sworn in before an Executive Magistrate/Notary Public.

Appendix-D

Form of Declaration (Municipal Corporation)

I, ... ,
S/o / D/o / W/o .... aged ....
years, a resident of Ward No. .... of ....
Municipal Corporation, Police Station ....
District ...., Bihar, declare:

that I am filing the nomination paper for election to the post of Ward Councillor of Ward No. .... of .... Municipal Corporation;

that I am fully conversant with the provisions of Section 14 of the Patna Municipal Corporation Act, 1951, as amended from time to time;

that I am not ineligible to be elected as a Ward Councillor or to continue as Ward Councillor after having been elected, under the provisions of Section 14 of the Patna Municipal Corporation Act, 1951, as amended from time to time; and

that the information furnished in the enclosed annexure are correct and true to the best of my knowledge and belief.

Signature of the Candidate

1. Full signature of witness -
   Address -

2. Full signature of witness -
   Address -

Place :

Date :

Appendix-D (*Contd.*)

Proforma for furnishing information under Section 14 of the Patna Municipal Corporation Act, 1951 by every candidate for election to the post of Ward Councillor of Municipal Corporation.

Election to the Ward Councillor of Ward No. .... of .... Municipal Corporation.

1. Name of the candidate —
2. Father's / Husband's name —
3. Have you ever been convicted by any court of law?
4. If the answer is yes, furnish the following information :
   (i) Name of the court by which convicted
   (ii) Date of conviction
   (iii) Nature of offence committed (with relevant Act/Sections)
   (iv) Punishment imposed
   (v) Period of imprisonment, if any
   (vi) Date of release from the prison
5. Has any appeal/review petition been filed against the above conviction
   (i) Details of appeal/review petition, if any
   (ii) Name of the court before which the appeal/review petition filed
   (iii) Whether appeal/review petition filed has been disposed of or pending
   (iv) If disposed of,
      (a) Date of disposal
      (b) Gist of the order passed
   (v) Whether bail granted during the pendency of the appeal/review petition
   (vi) If yes, the period during which remained on bail

Place : *Signature of the Candidate*
Date :

Appendix-E

Form of Declaration (Municipality)

I, ... ,
S/o / D/o / W/o .... aged ....
years, a resident of Ward No. .... of ....
.........Municipality, Police Station ....
District ...., Bihar, declare:

that I am filing the nomination paper for election to the post of Ward Commissioner of Ward No. .... of .... Municipality;

that I am fully conversant with the provisions of Section 17 of the Bihar Municipal Act, 1922, as amended from time to time;

that I am not ineligible to be elected as a Ward Commissioner or to continue as Ward Commissioner after having been elected, under the provisions of Section 17 of the Bihar Municipal Act, 1922, as amended from time to time; and

that the information furnished in the enclosed annexure are correct and true to the best of my knowledge and belief.

Signature of the Candidate

1. Full signature of witness -
   Address -
2. Full signature of witness -
   Address -

Place :
Date :

Appendix-E (*Contd.*)

Proforma for furnishing information under Section 17 of the Bihar Municipal Act, 1922 by every candidate for election to the post of Ward Commissioner of Municipality.

Election to the Ward Commissioner of Ward No. .... of .... Municipality.

1. Name of the candidate -
2. Father's/Husband's name -
3. Have you ever been convicted by any court of law?
4. If the answer is yes, furnish the following information :
   (i) Name of the court by which convicted
   (ii) Date of conviction
   (iii) Nature of offence committed (with relevant Act/Sections)
   (iv) Punishment imposed
   (v) Period of imprisonment, if any
   (vi) Date of release from the prison
5. Has any appeal/review petition been filed against the above conviction
   (i) Details of appeal/review petition, if any
   (ii) Name of the court before which the appeal/review petition filed
   (iii) Whether appeal/review petition filed has been disposed of or pending
   (iv) If disposed of,
      (a) Date of disposal
      (b) Gist of the order passed
   (v) Whether bail granted during the pendency of the appeal/review petition
   (vi) If yes, the period during which remained on bail

Place : *Signature of the Candidate*
Date :

Appendix-F

Decision of the Commission

Case No. 22/2002

Order

Dated 20.07.2002

[Under rule 122 of the Rules as amended with effect from 28.02.2002 read with sub-section (2) of Section 139 of the Act]

The brief facts of the case are that one Sri Krishna Murari Rai *alias* Murari Rai S/o Sri Sabrangi Rai was elected as Mukhiya of the Gram Panchayat Kalyanpur, Block Kalyanpur in the District of Samastipur in the general election to the three-tier Panchayat Institutions in the State held during April-May, 2001. Subsequently it came to light that the said Sri Krishna Murari Rai was convicted under Section 307/114 I.P.C. and was sentenced to undergo R.I. for seven years by the First Additional Sessions Judge, Samastipur *vide* order dated 06.09.1985 in the Sessions Trial No. 110/104 of 1986/1989 and accordingly the said Sri Krishna Murari Rai attracted the disqualification to contest election to the post of Mukhiya or Member of any Panchayat within the meaning of Section 139 (1) (g) of the Bihar Panchayat Raj Act, 1993 (Act). The relevant provisions of the above Section are extracted below:

> "(1) Notwithstanding anything contained in this Act, a person shall be disqualified for election or after election for holding the post as Mukhia, member of the Gram Panchayat, Sarpanch, Panch of the Gram Katchahri, member of the Panchayat Samiti and member of Zila Parishad, if such person—
>
> ....
>
> ....
>
> (g) Has been sentenced by a criminal court whether within or without Inda to imprisonment for an offence, other than a poltical offence, for a term

exceeding six months or has been ordered to furnish security for good behaviour under section 109 or section 110 of the Code of Criminal Procedure, 1973 (Act 2, 1974) and such sentence or order not having subsequently been reversed."

2. The question of disqualification as stated above is being decided in this case under rule 122 of the Rules, as amended with effect from 28.02.2002, read with sub-section (2) of Section 139 of the Act. Sub-section (2) of Section 139 and Rule 122 of the Rules are extracted below :

> "**Sub-section (2):** If any question arises as to whether a member of a Panchayat at any level has become subject to any of the disqualifications mentioned in Sub-section (1), the question shall be referred for the decision of such authority and in such manner as the Government may by law provide."

> "**Rule 122:** Under provisions of section 139 (2) of the Bihar Panchayat Raj Act, 1993, the State Election Commission shall be the competent authority to decide whether a member of a panchayat at any level has become subject to any of the disqualifications mentioned in Section 139(1) of the Act. The matter of disqualification may be brought to the notice of the State Election Commission in the form of a complaint, application or information by any person or authority. The State Election Commission may also take *suo motu* congnizance of such matters and decide such matters expeditiously after allowing sufficient opportunity to the affected parties of being heard."

3. Sri Krishna Murari Rai was present along with his advocate and he was heard on 04.07.2002 and also on 20.07.2002. He has also submitted written arguments. The implications of the provisions relating to disqualifications under Section 139(1) and (2) of the Act and rule 122 of the Rules were explained to them.

4. From a perusal of the records it would appear that Sri Krishna Murari Rai submitted his nomination for the post of Mukhiya of Kalyanpur Gram Panchayat before the Returning Officer on 14.02.2001 along with an affidavit in Schedule - II prescribed by the State Election Commission (Commission) in which he has stated that he is fully aware of the provisions of Section 139 of the Bihar Panchayat Raj Act, 1993 and that he is not ineligible to contest election for the post of Mukhiya and that having been elected to the post of Mukhiya he shall not be ineligible to hold the post of Mukhiya. It is clear that he has concealed the material information about his conviction and award of imprisonment for seven years by the Court of First Additional Sessions Judge, Samastipur as stated above which makes him disqualified to contest election for the post of Mukhiya under Section 139(1)(g) of the Act quoted above. It is clear that the said Sri Krishna Murari Rai has filed a false affidavit knowing fully well that the affidavit filed by him is false in so far as it relates to the provisions of disqualifications under Section 139 of the Act. Thus he was not eligible to file nomination for the post of Mukhiya of the Gram Panchayat Kalyanpur. Since he was not eligible to even contest the election, he is disqualified to hold the post of Mukhiya to which he was elected.

5. (i) During the course of hearing and also in the written arguments it was admitted that Sri Krishna Murari Rai has been sentenced to undergo R.I. for seven years by the court of First Additional Sessions Judge, Samastipur as indicated above. However, he pleaded that he has filed a Criminal Appeal No. 182/1995 in the Hon'ble High Court of Patna and he has produced a copy of the order dated 15.09.1995 of the Hon'ble Patna High Court. The Hon'ble High Court has not suspended the order of conviction passed by the Trial Court. However, the Hon'ble Patna High Court has directed that the accused Sri Krishna Murari Rai be released on bail. The submission of Sri Krishna Murari Rai is that since he has been granted bail by the Hon'ble Patna High Court he should not be treated as a convicted person till the High Court finally decides the case.

(ii) No doubt due to the fact that an appeal is pending in this case and hence no finality of the trial process has reached There is no denying the fact also that appeal is a continuation of the trial and that the judgements and orders passed by the Appellate Court upon an appeal shall be final except in certain cases as per provisions of Section 393 of the Cr.P.C. However, Sub-section (1)(g) of Section 139 of the Act makes it very clear that if the sentence of imprisonment for a term exceeding six months awarded by the Trial Court has not been subsequently reversed by any competent Court of law the concerned person continues to suffer from the disqualification provided therein. In the instant case bail has only been granted by the Hon'ble Patna High Court but the award of sentence has not been reversed or suspended and, therefore, said Sri Krishna Murari Rai suffers from the disqualification referred to in the Sub-section. Mere filing an appeal under Section 374 of Cr.P.C. would not automatically mean that the order of the Trial Court has been suspended. Sub-section (2) of Section 374 of the Cr.P.C. provides that any person convicted on a trial held by a Sessions Judge or an Additional Sessions Judge or by any other Court in which a sentence of imprisonment has been passed against him may appeal to the High Court. In the instant case Sri Krishna Murari Rai has availed of the legal remedy available to a convicted person under Section 374 Cr.P.C. and accordingly he has filed an appeal before the Hon'ble High Court of Patna. But the order of conviction and award of sentence for a term exceeding six months have not been suspended or reversed by any Court of law. Grant of bail alone, *ipso facto,* cannot be a ground to exclude Sri Krishna Murari Rai from the ambit of disqualification under Sub-section (1)(g) of Section 139 of the Act.

6. As regards the submission on behalf of Sri Krishna Murari Rai that in view of the order of the Hon'ble High Court granting him bail he should not be treated as a convicted person, it is relevant to analyse the provisions of Sub-section (1)(g) of Section 139 of the Act as quoted above. Sub-section (1)(g) makes it very clear that if a person has been sentenced by a Criminal Court, whether within or without India, to

imprisonment for an offence, other than a political offence, for a term exceeding six months and such sentence not having subsequently been reversed, such person shall be disqualified for election or after election for holding the post as Mukhiya of the Gram Panchayat. Thus as on date the order of conviction and the award of sentence for imprisonment for a period exceeding six months by a Criminal Court against Sri Krishna Murari Rai stands and that the above sentence has not been reversed till date. Therefore, the order of conviction and imprisonment for a period exceeding six months is legally and validly subsisting as on date in the eyes of law. Mere pendency of the Appeal before a Court cannot be a ground to exclude said Sri Krishna Murari Rai from the ambit of disqualifications within the meaning of Sub-section (1)(g) of Section 139 of the Act. So long the order of the Trial Court convicting him to undergo imprisonment for a period exceeding six months is not reversed by a competent court of law, the said Sri Krishna Murari Rai would continue to be disqualified for election to the post of Mukhiya of the Gram Panchayat and since he has already been elected to the said post, he shall be disqualified for holding the post of Mukhiya of Gram Panchayat Kalyanpur within the meaning of Sub-section (1) (g) of Section 139 of the Act.

7. During the course of hearing learned counsel also argued that since he has been enlarged on bail the provisions of Sub-section (1)(g) of Section 139 of the Act should not apply in his case. A reading of the above sub-section would make it clear that the two ingredients of the disqualification are that (i) a person has been sentenced by a Criminal Court to imprisonment for a term exceeding six months and that (ii) such sentence has not been subsequently reversed. Thus, Sub-section (1)(g) does not speak even of actual imprisonment to attract disqualification. A mere award of sentence to imprisonment (with or without actual imprisonment) for a term exceeding six months is adequate for the purpose of attracting disqualification if such sentence has not been subsequently reversed. In the instant case both the above two ingredients of the law are fulfilled and hence Sri Krishna

Murari Rai would attract the provision of disqualification of Sub-section (1)(g) of Section 139 of the Act.

8. It has been argued by the learned counsel of Sri Krishna Murari Rai that the instant proceedings does not lie against his client as he is not a Member of the Gram Panchayat, rather he is Mukhiya of the Gram Panchayat and as Mukhiya he is different from a Member of the Gram Panchayat. The argument of the learned counsel is that Sub-section (2) of Section 139 of the Act refers to the question of disqualification of a Member of a Panchayat and not of a Mukhiya, therefore, the instant proceedings is not maintainable against his client who is a Mukhiya. Sub-section (2) of Section 139 of the Act is to be read along with Sub-section (1) of the above Section. Sub-section (1) as quoted in page 1 of this order provides that a person shall be disqualified for election or after election for holding the post as Mukhiya or Member of the Gram Panchayat etc. if such person suffers from the disqualification under Sub-section (1)(g), i.e., conviction and sentence for a term exceeding six months and the sentence having subsequently not been reversed. Sub-section (2) refers to the disqualification mentioned in Sub-section (1) and hence the question of disqualification of a Member referred to in Sub-section (2) would also include the question of disqualification of a Mukhiya as Sub-section (1) and Sub-section (2) of Section 139 of the Act have to be read together and not in isolation. The learned counsel has referred to Section 12 of the Act to prove his point that Mukhiya is not a Member of the Panchayat. No doubt Mukhiya is elected directly by the voters of the entire Gram Panchayat area in the same manner as the Members of the Panchayat are directly elected by the voters of the respective wards. Thus the Mukhiya is a part of the Gram Panchayat and in a meeting of Panchayat he can exercise a casting vote when there is a tie and, therefore, he becomes first among the equals. The exclusive executive powers enjoyed by the Mukhiya under the Act or any scheme of the government does not mean that the Mukhiya is above the Panchayat and that a Mukhiya is not part of the Panchayat. Therefore, the contention of the learned counsel that Mukhiya

is not a Member of the Gram Panchayat cannot be sustained. Similarly, the contention of the learned counsel that instant proceedings does not lie against his client also cannot be sustained for the reasons stated above.

9. The learned counsel has also referred to Rule 122 of the Bihar Panchayat Election Rules, 1995 (Rules) and has argued that the present proceedings lies before the concerned Munsiff Magistrate and not before the Commission. The learned counsel was shown government notification No. 657/GP dated 28.02.2002 by which the old Rule 122 has been substituted by a new rule under which the Commission has been declared as the competent authority to decide such matter. The learned counsel has accepted the legal position as above.

10. Learned counsel has informed that the Hon'ble High Court of Patna has agreed to consider the Criminal Appeal filed by his client and it is expected that the Hon'ble High Court would hear the Criminal Appeal early and, therefore, the learned counsel said that this case may be kept pending. Sri Krishna Murari Rai has filed a Criminal Appeal before the Hon'ble High Court at Patna and the appeal is pending for disposal. Thus as on date no final decision has been taken in the appeal and, therefore, the order of conviction and sentence passed by the Lower Court has not been reversed by any competent court of law and hence Sri Krishna Murari Rai continues to suffer from the disqualification within the meaning of Section 139(1)(g) of the Act. The request of the learned counsel for time is not justified and hence the same is rejected.

11. Now the question is whether the election of Sri Krishna Murari Rai as Mukhiya of Gram Panchayat Kalyanpur shall subsist or not in view of the fact that (i) he was disqualified to file nomination for the post of Mukhiya and that (ii) his nomination itself was fit to be rejected as he was disqualified to contest the election. It is proved that Sri Krishna Murari Rai was disqualified to file nomination and, therefore, he was even not eligible to contest the election. The fact that his nomination was accepted by the Returning Officer in the

absence of any knowledge about his disqualification and on the strength of a false affidavit filed by Sri Krishna Murari Rai does not take away the disqualification he suffers from under Section 139 (1) (g) of the Act. Consequently, Sri Krishna Murari Rai cannot continue in the post of Mukhiya of Gram Panchayat Kalyanpur as being disqualified for the reasons stated above.

12. Under the circumstances stated above, the State Election Commission, in exercise of its power under Rule 122 of the Rules read with Sub-section (2) of Section 139 of the Act, hereby orders that Sri Krishna Murari Rai, who was disqualified for election to the post of Mukhiya of Gram Panchayat Kalyanpur but was elected to the said post on the strength of invalid nomination, shall be disqualified for holding the post of Mukhiya of Gram Panchayat Kalyanpur within the meaning of Sub-section (1)(g) of Section 139 of the Act. In other words, the said Sri Krishna Murari Rai shall cease to hold the post of Mukhiya of Gram Panchayat Kalyanpur and to function as such Mukhiya. The post of Mukhiya of Gram Panchayat Kalyanpur shall, accordingly, be deemed to be vacant. The function of the Mukhiya of the Gram Panchayat Kalyanpur shall be discharged in accordance with the relevant provisions of the Act till the vacancy in the post of Mukhiya of Gram Panchayat Kalyanpur is filled in accordance with the provisions of the Act.

13. This order shall take effect from the date of its receipt by the Block Development Officer, Kalyanpur.

Appendix-G

Decision of the Commission

Case No. 73/2002

Order

Dated 17.09.2002

[Under rule 122 of the Rules as amended with effect from 28.02.2002 read with Sub-section (2) of Section 139 of the Act]

The brief facts of the case are that one Sri Shailendra Mahto S/o Sri Krishna Singh was elected as Mukhiya of the Gram Panchayat Barandi, Block Rahui in the District of Nalanda in the general election to the three-tier Panchayat Institutions in the State held during April-May, 2001. Subsequently it came to light that the said Sri Shailendra Mahto was convicted under Section 302/34 I.P.C. and was sentenced to undergo life imprisonment by the 2nd Additional Sessions Judge, Nalanda, Biharsharif *vide* order dated 22.02.1988 in the Sessions Trial No. 258/86/10/87 and accordingly the said Sri Shailendra Mahto attracted the disqualification to contest election to the post of Mukhiya or Member of any Panchayat within the meaning of Section 139 (1) (g) of the Bihar Panchayat Raj Act, 1993 (Act). The relevant provisions of the above Section are extracted below:

> "(1) Notwithstanding anything contained in this Act, a person shall be disqualified for election or after election for holding the post as Mukhiya, member of the Gram Panchayat, Sarpanch, Panch of the Gram Katchahri, member of the Panchayat Samiti and member of Zila Parishad, if such person—
>
> ....
>
> ....
>
> (g) Has been sentenced by a criminal court whether within or without Inda to imprisonment for an

offence, other than a political offence, for a term exceeding six months or has been ordered to furnish security for good behaviour under Section 109 or Section 110 of the Code of Criminal Procedure, 1973 (Act 2, 1974) and such sentence or order not having subsequently been reversed."

2. The question of disqualification as stated above is being decided in this case under Rule 122 of the Rules, as amended with effect from 28.02.2002, read with Sub-section (2) of Section 139 of the Act. Sub-section (2) of Section 139 and Rule 122 of the Rules are extracted below:

> "**Sub-section (2)** : If any question arises as to whether a member of a Panchayat at any level has become subject to any of the disqualifications mentioned in sub-section (1), the question shall be referred for the decision of such authority and in such manner as the Government may by law provide."

> "**Rule 122** : Under provisions of Section 139(2) of the Bihar Panchayat Raj Act, 1993, the State Election Commission shall be the competent authority to decide whether a member of a Panchayat at any level has become subject to any of the disqualifications mentioned in Section 139(1) of the Act. The matter of disqualification may be brought to the notice of the State Election Commission in the form of a complaint, application or information by any person or authority. The State Election Commission may also take *suo motu* cognizance of such matters and decide such matters expeditiously after allowing sufficient opportunity to the affected parties of being heard."

3. From a perusal of the records it would appear that Sri Shailendra Mahto, opposite party (O.P.) in this case submitted his nomination for the post of Mukhiya of Barandi Gram Panchayat before the Returning Officer on 17.02.2001 along

with an affidavit in Schedule-II prescribed by the State Election Commission (Commission) in which he has stated that he is fully aware of the provisions of Section 139 of the Bihar Panchayat Raj Act, 1993 and that he is not ineligible to contest election for the post of Mukhiya and that having been elected to the post of Mukhiya he shall not be ineligible to hold the post of Mukhiya. It is clear that he has concealed the material information about his conviction and award of life imprisonment by the Court of Second Additional Sessions Judge, Nalanda as stated above which makes him disqualified to contest election for the post of Mukhiya under Section 139(1)(g) of the Act quoted above. It is clear that said Sri Shailendra Mahto has filed a false affidavit knowing fully well that the affidavit filed by him is false in so far as it relates to the provisions of disqualifications under Section 139 of the Act. Thus he was not eligible to file nomination for the post of Mukhiya of the Gram Panchayat Barandi. Since he was not eligible to even contest the election, he is disqualified to hold the post of Mukhiya to which he was elected.

4. Sri Shailendra Mahto, Opposite Party (O.P.) in this case, was absent on all the occasions. He was, however, represented by his learned counsel who was heard. The O.P. was granted time earlier also but he could not produce any relevant document in his support. Again on 10.09.2002 a petition was filed on behalf of the O.P. on the ground that he is ill. It is clear that the O.P. has been trying to avoid appearance before the Commission. In the absence of any documentary evidence or oral evidence the order of conviction and sentence for life imprisonment under Section 302 and 34 I.P.C. passed against the O.P. by the Second Additional Sessions Judge, Nalanda, on 22.02.88 in Sessions Trial No. 258 of 1986/10 of 1987 stands.

5. Written arguments were filed on behalf of the O.P. It has been argued that the Commission has no jurisdiction to continue with the instant proceeding as its role ends with the completion of election. It has also been argued that proper course in such case is to file an election petition before the competent authority. This issue has been dealt with in detail later in this order. However, it is relevant to mention here

that the Commission is considering the question of disqualification of the O.P. under Rule 122 of the Bihar Panchayat Election Rules, 1995 as substituted with effect from 28.02.2002 under which the Commission has full jurisdiction to decide the matter in the instant case. It has further been argued that until the appeal filed by the O.P. is finally decided, he will be treated as innocent and, therefore, the order of conviction and sentence passed against the O.P. by the Trial Court cannot operate. Although the learned counsel has not indicated the details of the Criminal Appeal filed by his client, it is presumed that the O.P. has filed an appeal against the order of conviction and sentence passed by the Second Additional Sessions Judge, Nalanda *vide* its order dated 22.02.88. However, from the records of Case No. 72/2002 involving one Sri Indrajeet Prasad who is a co-accused along with the O.P. it is noticed that the accused has filed a Criminal Appeal No. 183/88 before the Hon'ble High Court at Patna and the Hon'ble High Court *vide* its order dated 27.05.88 has admitted the appeal for hearing and has directed that the O.P. be released on bail. There is nothing on record to show that the above Criminal Appeal has been finally decided by the Hon'ble High Court. The status of an accused who has filed an appeal has been clarified by the Hon'ble Supreme Court *vide* its order dated 21.09.2001 referred to in detail later in this order. The Supreme Court has clarified that until the order of conviction and sentence is set aside in appeal the accused cannot be treated as innocent and, therefore, the relevant disqualification would continue to apply in his case.

6. It has been argued by the learned counsel that the instant proceeding is not maintainable before the Commission and the appropriate remedy is to file an election petition before the prescribed authority. It is relevant to mention here that the Commission is not hearing any election petition as it is not competent to do so. An election can be declared as void by the prescribed authority, in this case the concerned Munsif Magistrate, on various grounds as enumerated under Section 144 of the Act. Besides the question of disqualification under the Act, there are other grounds including corrupt practices,

for which the Munsif Magistrate can declare the election itself as void. The question for decision before the Commission is whether the said Sri Shailendra Mahto suffers from the disqualification under Sub-section (1)(g) of Section 139 of the Act. This power has been delegated to the Commission under Rule 122 of the Bihar Panchayat Election Rules, 1995 (Rules) as notified by the Government *vide* No. 2Pa/VI3-444/2001/657/G.P. dated 28th February, 2002 under the provisions of Sub-section (2) of Section 139 of the Act. The Commission is exercising the power vested in it under Rule 122 of the Rules read with Sub-section (2) of Section 139 of the Act. Thus the issue for decision before the Commission is different from the issue to be decided in an election petition by the competent court of law. The Commission is, therefore, perfectly justified in deciding the question of disqualification, if any, of any person under Rule 122 read with Sub-section (2) of Section 139 of the Act. Hence the above submission cannot be sustained.

7. (i) The O.P. Sri Shailendra Mahto was convicted and sentenced to life imprisonment by the Second Addl. Sessions Judge, Nalanda under Section 302/34 I.P.C. *vide* order dated 22.02.1988 in Sessions Trial No. 258/1986/10/1987. No document has been produced to establish that the order of conviction and sentence passed by the Trial Court as indicated above has been set aside by any Appellate Court. Therefore, the O.P. Sri Shailendra Mahto would suffer from the disqualification within the meaning of clause (g) of Sub-section (1) of Section 139 of the Act until the order of conviction and sentence is set aside by a competent court in appeal as per the ruling of the Hon'ble Supreme Court of India in Writ Petitions (C) No. 242 of 2001 with others decided on 21.09.2001 in B. R. Kapur *Vs.* State of Tamil Nadu & Another reproduced in (2001) 7 Supreme Court Cases 231. Para 40 and 44 of the above judgement have extensively dealt with this question by the Hon'ble Supreme Court. The Supreme Court has clarified that when a lower court convicts an accused and sentences him, the presumption that the accused is innocent comes to an end. The conviction operates and the accused has to undergo the

sentence. The execution of the sentence can be stayed by the Appellate Court and the accused released on bail. If the appeal of the accused succeeds the conviction is wiped out as cleanly as if it had never existed. A successful appeal means that the stigma of the offence is altogether erased. But it does not mean that the presumption of innocence continues after the conviction by the Trial Court. The order of conviction and the award of sentence it carries, operate against the accused in all their rigour until set aside in appeal and a disqualification that attaches to the conviction and sentence shall apply equally. In other words, until the order of conviction and sentence are set aside in the Criminal Appeal pending before the Hon'ble High Court the order of conviction and the order of sentence shall operate and consequently the disqualification provided under clause (g) of Sub-section (1) of Section 139 of the Act shall continue to apply in the case of the O.P. In the present case the Criminal Appeal is pending before the Hon'ble High Court and until the order of the Trial Court is set aside the O.P. cannot be excluded from the ambit of disqualification under the Act. The above aspect has been more forcefully clarified by the Hon'ble Supreme Court in para 44 of the judgement referred to above. It has been clarified that there can be no doubt that in a criminal case acquittal in appeal takes effect retrospectively and wipes out the sentence awarded by lower court. This implies that the stigma attached to the conviction and rigour of sentence are completely obliterated. But it does not mean that the effect of conviction and sentence of the lower court is obliterated until the order of conviction and sentence are set aside by the Appellate Court. The conviction and sentence operate pending decision on the appeal for the purpose of the disqualifications provided for under Sub-section (1) of Section 139 of the Act in the case of the O.P. This will be further clear from the reading of clause (g) of Sub-section (1) of Section 139 of the Act. The above clause does not refer to actual imprisonment of the accused as many times the Trial Court may convict and sentence the accused and also may grant provisional bail instantly to allow the accused to file an appeal and it is quite possible that the provisional bail granted by the Trial Court is confirmed by the Appellate Court. Thus the order of conviction and sentence for a term exceeding six months, with or without actual imprisonment, is adequate for the purpose of attracting provision of disqualification provided for in the above sub-clause.

(ii) The O.P. could not produce any documentary evidence or even oral evidence to prove that the order of conviction and sentence passed by the Second Addl. Sessions Judge, Nalanda as referred to above has been reversed by any competent court of law. That being so the O.P. suffers from the disqualification within the meaning of clause (g) of Sub-section (1) of Section 139 of the Act.

(iii) Under the circumstances stated in sub-paras (i) and (ii) above, the O.P. would continue to suffer from the disqualification provided for in clause (g) of Sub-section (1) of Section 139 of the Act until the order of the Trial Court convicting and sentencing him for a term exceeding six months is set aside by the Appellate Court.

8. Now the question is whether Sri Shailendra Mahto shall be qualified to hold the post of Mukhiya of Gram Panchayat Barandi or not in view of the fact that (i) he was disqualified to file nomination for the post of Mukhiya and that (ii) his nomination itself was fit to be rejected as he was disqualified to contest the election. It has been proved that Sri Shailendra Mahto was disqualified to file nomination and, therefore, he was even not eligible to contest the election. The fact that his nomination was accepted by the Returning Officer in the absence of any knowledge about his disqualification and on the strength of a false affidavit filed by Sri Shailendra Mahto does not take away the disqualification he suffers from under Section 139(1)(g) of the Act. Consequently, Sri Shailendra Mahto cannot continue in the post of Mukhiya of Gram Panchayat Barandi as being disqualified for the reasons stated above.

9. Under the circumstances stated above, the State Election Commission, in exercise of its power under Rule 122 of the Rules read with Sub-section (2) of Section 139 of the Act,

hereby orders that Sri Shailendra Mahto, who was disqualified for election to the post of Mukhiya of Gram Panchayat Barandi but was elected to the said post on the strength of invalid nomination, shall be disqualified for holding the post of Mukhiya of Gram Panchayat Barandi within the meaning of Sub-section (1) (g) of Section 139 of the Act. In other words, the said Sri Shailendra Mahto shall cease to hold the post of Mukhiya of Gram Panchayat Barandi and to function as such Mukhiya. The post of Mukhiya of Gram Panchayat Barandi shall, accordingly, be deemed to be vacant. The function of the Mukhiya of the Gram Panchayat Barandi shall be discharged in accordance with the relevant provisions of the Act till the vacancy in the post of Mukhiya of Gram Panchayat Barandi is filled in accordance with the provisions of the Act.

10. This order shall take effect from the date of its receipt by the Block Development Officer, Rahui.

Appendix-H

Decision of the Commission

Case No. 31/2002

Order

Dated 25.09.2002

[Under Rule 122 of the Rules as amended with effect from 28.02.2002 read with Sub-section (2) of Section 139 of the Act]

The brief facts of the case are that one Sri Rajendra Prasad Sharma *alias* Awadhesh Sharma S/o Sri Jayashree Sharma was elected as Mukhiya of the Gram Panchayat Sahar Telpa, Block Karpi in the District of Arwal in the general election to the three-tier Panchayat Institutions in the State held during April-May, 2001. Subsequently it came to light that the said Sri Rajendra Prasad Sharma was convicted under Section 25/26/35 Arms Act and was sentenced to undergo imprisonment for 2 years by the Judicial Magistrate, First Class, Jahanabad (now Arwal) *vide* order dated 26.02.2001 in Trial No. 60/2001 (GR No. 396/96) and accordingly the said Sri Rajendra Prasad Sharma attracted the disqualification to contest election to the post of Mukhiya or Member of any Panchayat within the meaning of Section 139 (1) (g) of the Bihar Panchayat Raj Act, 1993 (Act). The relevant provisions of the above Section are extracted below:

> "(1) Notwithstanding anything contained in this Act, a person shall be disqualified for election or after election for holding the post as Mukhiya, member of the Gram Panchayat, Sarpanch, Panch of the Gram Katchahri, member of the Panchayat Samiti and member of Zila Parishad, if such person—
>
> ....
>
> ....

(g) Has been sentenced by a criminal court whether within or without Inda to imprisonment for an offence, other than a political offence, for a term exceeding six months or has been ordered to furnish security for good behaviour under Section 109 or Section 110 of the Code of Criminal Procedure, 1973 (Act 2, 1974) and such sentence or order not having subsequently been reversed."

2. The question of disqualification as stated above is being decided in this case under Rule 122 of the Rules, as amended with effect from 28.02.2002, read with Sub-section (2) of Section 139 of the Act. Sub-section (2) of Section 139 and Rule 122 of the Rules are extracted below:

"**Sub-section (2)** : If any question arises as to whether a member of a Panchayat at any level has become subject to any of the disqualifications mentioned in Sub-section (1), the question shall be referred for the decision of such authority and in such manner as the Government may by law provide."

"**Rule 122** : Under provisions of Section 139(2) of the Bihar Panchayat Raj Act, 1993, the State Election Commission shall be the competent authority to decide whether a member of a Panchayat at any level has become subject to any of the disqualifications mentioned in Section 139(1) of the Act. The matter of disqualification may be brought to the notice of the State Election Commission in the form of a complaint, application or information by any person or authority. The State Election Commission may also take *suo motu* congnizance of such matters and decide such matters expeditiously after allowing sufficient opportunity to the affected parties of being heard."

3. From a perusal of the records it would appear that Sri Rajendra Prasad Sharma submitted his nomination for the

post of Mukhiya of Sahar Telpa Gram Panchayat before the Returning Officer on 23.02.2001 along with an affidavit in Schedule-II prescribed by the State Election Commission (Commission) in which he has stated that he is fully aware of the provisions of Section 139 of the Bihar Panchayat Raj Act, 1993 and that he is not ineligible to contest election for the post of Mukhiya and that having been elected to the post of Mukhiya he shall not be ineligible to hold the post of Mukhiya. The affidavit filed by Sri Rajendra Prasad Sharma, Opposite Party (O.P.) in this case, was true on the date of submitting the same on 23.02.2001 to the Returning Officer along with the nomination paper. However, it so happened that the Judicial Magistrate First Class, Jahanabad passed an order on 26.02.2001 by which the O.P. was convicted and sentenced to two years' imprisonment as indicated above. The O.P. should have withdrawn from the election by a separate communication to the Returning Officer indicating the circumstances (order of conviction and sentence) to the Returning Officer. Thus even though he did not suffer from the disqualification under clause (g) of Sub-section (1) of Section 139 on the date of filing the nomination he became disqualified immediately thereafter and, therefore, the O.P. should have withdrawn from the election. The election for Karpi Block was scheduled during the fifth phase when voting was to take place on 27.04.2001. The last date for filing nomination was 26.02.2001 and the date of scrutiny of the nomination was 27.02.2001 and the last date for withdrawal of nomination was 28.02.2001. Therefore, the O.P. had enough time to withdraw his candidature. In fact he has filed the Criminal Appeal on 26.02.2001, on the same date when the Trial Court passed the order and he should have shown the same promptness in withdrawing his candidature for which he had enough time to do so.

4. The O.P. was present during hearing on all the occasions. He was also present along with his Advocate twice and they were heard and the implications of Sub-section (1) of Section 139 was explained to them. It is admitted that the O.P. has been convicted and sentenced to imprisonment for two years

as indicated above. The O.P. has filed a Criminal Appeal No. 14/2001 before the District and Sessions Judge. The Criminal Appeal has been admitted for hearing on 26.02.2001, i.e., on the same day when the order of conviction and sentence was passed by the Trial Court. While admitting the Criminal Appeal, the Appellate Court has confirmed the provisional bail granted to the O.P. by the Trial Court. The Criminal Appeal is pending decision. During the course of hearing both the O.P. and his learned counsel pleaded for time so as to enable the O.P. to obtain a Stay Order from the Appellate Court. Accordingly, time was granted but till the last date of hearing on 19.09.2002 the O.P. could not produce any order to that effect. The O.P. was present in person on 19.09.2002 and he stated that the case was coming before the Appellate Court on 19.09.2002 and it is expected that the order will be passed. In this case the O.P. was given adequate opportunity to produce a favourable order from the Appellate Court. It is not, however, possible to adjourn the case indefinitely till the final order in the Appeal. Nevertheless the O.P. was told that final order in this case will be passed on 23.09.2002 and if the O.P. could produce any order passed by the Appellate Court in his favour by 23.09.2002 the same will be considered while passing the final order. It was made clear to the O.P. that no further time will be given beyond 23.09.2002.

5. The O.P. Sri Rajendra Prasad Sharma *alias* Awadhesh Sharma, elected Mukhiya of Sahar Telpa Gram Panchayat of Karpi Block in the District of Arwal has submitted a certified copy of the order dated 21.09.2002 passed by the District and Sessions Judge, Jahanabad in Criminal Appeal No. 14/2001 filed by the O.P. against the order dated 26.02.2001 passed by the Judicial Magistrate First Class, Jahanabad sentencing the O.P. to two years imprisonment as quoted above. A petition was filed by one Sri Baidyanath Thakur, Advocate on 23.09.2002 stating therein that the Appellate Court has not set aside the order of the Trial Court as claimed by the O.P. He has not filed any *vakalatnama* and, therefore, it is not clear as to whom the learned counsel was representing. Apparently this has been done on behalf of some prospective intervener. Since no

document has been produced to contradict the judgement of the Appellate Court, a certified copy of which has been produced by the O.P., no credence can be given to such petition filed by the Advocate and, therefore, the same is ignored.

6. From a perusal of the order of the Appellate Court it is clear that the Appellate Court has acquitted the O.P. *vide* his order dated 21.09.2002 in Criminal Appeal No. 14/2001. Thus with the order of acquittal passed by the Appellate Court referred to above, the order of conviction and sentence by the Trial Court is wiped out as cleanly as if it has never existed and accordingly the stigma of the offence and the consequent disqualification under clause (g) of Sub-section (1) of Section 139 of the Act is altogether erased in terms of the order of the Hon'ble Supreme Court in Writ Petitions (c) No. 242 of 2001 with others decided on 21.09.2001 in B.R. Kapur *Vs.* State of Tamil Nadu and Another reproduced in (2001) 7 Supreme Court cases 231 (*vide* para 40 and 44).

7. Under the circumstances stated above, the State Election Commission in exercise of its power under Rule 122 of the Rules read with Sub-section (2) of section 139 of the Act hereby orders that Sri Rajendra Prasad Sharma shall be qualified to hold the post of Mukhiya of the Gram Panchayat Sahar Telpa to which he was duly elected during the general election held in April-May, 2001.

Appendix-I

Decision of the Commission

Case No. 91/2002

Order

Dated 09.12.2002

[Under Rule 122 of the Rules as amended with effect from 28.02.2002 read with Sub-section (2) of Section 139 of the Act]

The brief facts of the this case are that one Sri Ramakant Dubey son of Late Ram Bachan Dubey of village Khandhara Pandeypur, P.S. Simari in the district of Buxar (petitioner in this case) filed a petition alleging that one Sri Satya Narayan Dubey son of Sri Harkhu Dubey of the same village and district (Opposite Party in this case), who was elected as a Member of the Simari Panchayat Samiti, has been sentenced to imprisonment for life under Section 302 IPC by the Sessions Judge, Buxar *vide* his order dated 18.07.2002 in Sessions Trial No. 38 of 1979 and accordingly the Opposite Party (OP) attracted the disqualification to hold the post of a Member of the Panchayat Samiti within the meaning of Section 139(1)(g) of the Bihar Panchayat Raj Act, 1993 (Act). The relevant provisions of the above section are extracted below :

> "(1) Notwithstanding anything contained in this Act, a person shall be disqualified for election or after election for holding the post as Mukhyia, member of the Gram Panchayat, Sarpanch, Panch of the Gram Katchahri, member of the Panchayat Samiti and member of Zila Parishad, if such person—
>
> ....
>
> ....
>
> (g) Has been sentenced by a criminal court whether within or without Inda to imprisonment for an offence, other than a political offence, for a term

exceeding six months or has been ordered to furnish security for good behaviour under Section 109 or Section 110 of the Code of Criminal Procedure, 1973 (Act 2, 1974) and such sentence or order not having subsequently been reversed."

2. The question of disqualification as stated above is being decided in this case under rule 122 of the Rules, as amended with effect from 28.02.2002, read with Sub-section (2) of Section 139 of the Act. Sub-section (2) of Section 139 and Rule 122 of the Rules are extracted below:

"**Sub-section (2):** If any question arises as to whether a member of a Panchayat at any level has become subject to any of the disqualifications mentioned in Sub-section (1), the question shall be referred for the decision of such authority and in such manner as the Government may by law provide."

"**Rule 122** : Under provisions of Section 139(2) of the Bihar Panchayat Raj Act, 1993, the State Election Commission shall be the competent authority to decide whether a member of a panchayat at any level has become subject to any of the disqualifications mentioned in Section 139(1) of the Act. The matter of disqualification may be brought to the notice of the State Election Commission in the form of a complaint, application or information by any person or authority. The State Election Commission may also take *suo motu* congnizance of such matters and decide such matters expeditiously after allowing sufficient opportunity to the affected parties of being heard."

3. Show cause has been filed on behalf of the O.P. The petitioner and the O.P. were represented by their advocates who were heard. The facts admitted in this case are that the O.P. was elected as a Member of Simari Panchayat Samiti in

the election to the three-tier Panchayat Institutions in Bihar during April-May, 2001 and at that point of time the O.P. was not a convicted person and that the O.P. was convicted by the Sessions Judge, Buxar referred to above on 18.07.2002.

4. The learned counsel of the O.P. has argued that since the O.P. did not attract the disqualification under clause (g) of Sub-section (1) of Section 139 of the Act at the time of filing his nomination and also at the time of his election as a Member of the Panchayat Samiti, the petition is fit to be rejected. In this connection, he has also referred to the order passed by the State Election Commission in Case No. 30/2002 in which *vide* its order dated 02.07.2002 the Commission has exonerated one elected representative of a Gram Panchayat under similar circumstances. In this connection, it will be relevant to examine the implications of Sub-section (1) and Sub-section (2) of Section 139 of the Act before coming to a conclusion if decision taken by the Commission in the past referred to above could be binding on this case also or the decision taken in the above noted case earlier would be in the nature of an *obiter dictum*, i.e., not binding on all cases.

5. Sub-section (1) of Section 139 of the Act quoted above clearly stipulates that a person shall be disqualified for election as a Mukhiya or Member of a Panchayat if he suffers from any of the disqualifications mentioned therein. In other words, a person who suffers from any of the disqualifications shall not be eligible to contest the elections. The second part of Sub-section (1) goes further and provides that such a disqualified person, if elected, shall be disqualified for holding the post to which he was eventually elected, his disqualification notwithstanding. Thus provision of Sub-section (1) would apply not only in respect of a person who suffers from any of the specified disqualifications prior to the election or at the time of election but also in respect of a person who manages to get himself elected in the absence of his disqualification being detected by the Returning Officer at the time of scrutiny so that he cannot escape the arm of the law.

6. Sub-section (2) of Section 139 of the Act quoted above provides that if any question arises as to whether a Member

of a Panchayat at any level has become subject to any of the disqualifications mentioned in Sub-section (1) the question shall be decided by the appropriate authority. Clearly this Sub-section refers to a Member of a Panchayat, i.e., a person who has been elected as a Member of a Panchayat and has become subject to any of the disqualifications mentioned in Sub-section (1). Thus when the question of disqualification comes up before the appropriate authority for decision, the appropriate authority has necessarily to read Sub-section (1) and Sub-section (2) together and not in isolation. As observed in the preceding para, Sub-section (1) would give a reasonable impression that the disqualifications specified therein would be relevant for a person who has incurred the disqualification before election. But a reading of Sub-section (2) would also give an equally clear understanding that the disqualification would also be relevant in respect of a person incurring such disqualifications after election. This Sub-section speaks of a "*Member*" of a Panchayat being subject to any of the disqualifications. Obviously, to be a "*Member*" of a Panchayat one has to contest election and get elected as such and, therefore, this sub-section refers to a post-election scenario. As regards the expression "*has become*" subject to any of the disqualifications the same should also be understood as "*is*" subject to any of the disqualifications.

7. From what has been stated in the preceding two paragraphs it would be clear that Sub-section (1) and Sub-section (2) of Section 139 of the Act should be read together and not in isolation and, therefore, any person, whether disqualified before election or after election, would fall within the ambit of the provisions of Sub-section (2) and accordingly the question of disqualification of any such person shall be dealt with accordingly. The order passed by the Commission in Case No. 30/2002 referred to above is in the nature of an *obiter dictum* without any binding authority on other cases. To put simply, an incorrect assessment of the legal provisions in one case cannot be binding in another case subsequently and the Commission cannot review its own order passed in a particular case as being *functus officio*.

8. The learned counsel of the O.P. has argued that since his client has been granted bail by the Hon'ble High Court at Patna *vide* its order dated 31.07.2002 in Criminal Appeal No. 455/2002 (DB) the O.P. should not be treated as a convicted person till the appeal is finally disposed of. No doubt due to the fact that an appeal is pending in this case and hence no finality of the trial process has reached. There is no denying the fact also that appeal is a continuation of the trial and that the judgements and orders passed by the Appellate Court upon an appeal shall be final except in certain cases as per provisions of Section 393 of the Cr.P.C. However, Sub-section (1)(g) of Section 139 of the Act makes it very clear that if the sentence of imprisonment for a term exceeding six months awarded by the Trial Court has not been subsequently reversed by any competent Court of law the concerned person continues to suffer from the disqualification provided therein. In the instant case bail has only been granted by the Hon'ble Patna High Court but the award of sentence has not been reversed and, therefore, the said O.P. suffers from the disqualification referred to in the Sub-section. Mere filing an appeal under Section 374 of Cr.P.C. would not automatically mean that the order of the Trial Court has been reversed. Sub-section (2) of Section 374 of the Cr.P.C. provides that any person convicted on a trial held by a Sessions Judge or an Additional Sessions Judge or by any other Court in which a sentence of imprisonment for more than 7 years has been passed against him may appeal to the High Court. In the instant case the O.P. has availed of the legal remedy available to a convicted person under Section 374 Cr.P.C. and accordingly he has filed an appeal before the Hon'ble High Court of Patna. But the order of conviction and award of sentence for a term exceeding six months have not been reversed by any court of law. Grant of bail alone, *ipso facto,* cannot be a ground to exclude the O.P. from the ambit of disqualification under Sub-section (1)(g) of Section 139 of the Act.

9. As regards the submission on behalf of the O.P. that in view of the order of the Hon'ble High Court granting him

bail he should not be treated as a convicted person, it is relevant to analyse the provisions of Sub-section (1)(g) of Section 139 of the Act as quoted above. Sub-section (1)(g) makes it very clear that if a person has been sentenced by a Criminal Court, whether within or without India, to imprisonment for an offence, other than a political offence, for a term exceeding six months and such sentence not having subsequently been reversed, such person shall be disqualified for election or after election for holding the post as Mukhiya of the Gram Panchayat or as member of a Panchayat. Thus as on date the order of conviction and the award of sentence for imprisonment for a period exceeding six months by a Criminal Court against the O.P. stands and that the above sentence has not been reversed till date. Therefore, the order of conviction and imprisonment for a period exceeding six months is legally and validly subsisting as on date in the eyes of law. Mere pendency of an Appeal before a Court cannot be a ground to exclude the said O.P. from the ambit of disqualifications within the meaning of Sub-section (1)(g) of Section 139 of the Act. So long the order of the Trial Court convicting him to undergo imprisonment for a period exceeding six months is not reversed by a competent court of law, the said O.P. would continue to be disqualified for election to the post of a member of a Panchayat and since he has already been elected to the said post, he shall be disqualified for holding the post of member of Simari Panchayat Samiti within the meaning of Sub-section (1)(g) of Section 139 of the Act.

10. During the course of hearing the learned counsel of the O.P. has also argued that since the O.P. has been released on bail the provisions of Sub-section (1)(g) of Section 139 of the Act should not apply in his case. A reading of the above Sub-section would make it clear that the two ingredients of the disqualification are that (i) a person has been sentenced by a Criminal Court to imprisonment for a term exceeding six months and that (ii) such sentence has not been subsequently reversed. Thus, Sub-section (1)(g) does not speak even of actual imprisonment to attract disqualification. A mere award of sentence to imprisonment (with or without

actual imprisonment) for a term exceeding six months is adequate for the purpose of attracting disqualification if such sentence has not been subsequently reversed. In the instant case both the above two ingredients of the law are fulfilled and hence the O.P. would attract the provision of disqualification of Sub-section (1)(g) of Section 139 of the Act.

11. It is clear that the O.P. was convicted and sentenced to life imprisonment by the Sessions Judge, Buxar as stated above. No document has been produced to establish that the order of conviction and sentence passed by the Trial Court as indicated above has been set aside by any Appellate Court. Therefore, the O.P. would suffer from the disqualification within the meaning of clause (g) of Sub-section (1) of Section 139 of the Act until the order of conviction and sentence is set aside by a competent court in appeal as per the ruling of the Hon'ble Supreme Court of India in Writ Petition (C) No. 242 of 2001 with others decided on 21.09.2001 in B. R. Kapur *Vs.* State of Tamil Nadu & Another reproduced in (2001) 7 Supreme Court Cases 231. Para 40 and para 44 of the above judgement have extensively dealt with this question by the Hon'ble Supreme Court. The Supreme Court has clarified that when a lower court convicts an accused and sentences him, the presumption that the accused is innocent comes to an end. The conviction operates and the accused has to undergo the sentence. The execution of the sentence can be stayed by the Appellate Court and the accused released on bail. If the appeal of the accused succeeds the conviction is wiped out as cleanly as if it had never existed. A successful appeal means that the stigma of the offence is altogether erased. But it does not mean that the presumption of innocence continues after the conviction by the Trial Court. The order of conviction and the award of sentence it carries, operate against the accused in all their rigour until set aside in appeal and a disqualification that attaches to the conviction and sentence shall apply equally. In other words, until the order of conviction and sentence are set aside in the Criminal Appeal pending before the Hon'ble High Court the order of conviction and the order of sentence shall operate and consequently the disqualification

provided under clause (g) of Sub-section (1) of Section 139 of the Act shall continue to apply in the case of the O.P. In the present case, the Criminal Appeal is pending before the Hon'ble High Court and until the order of the Trial Court is set aside the O.P. cannot be excluded from the ambit of disqualification under the Act. The above aspect has been more forcefully clarified by the Hon'ble Supreme Court in para 44 of the judgement referred to above. It has been clarified that there can be no doubt that in a criminal case acquittal in appeal takes effect retrospectively and wipes out the sentence awarded by lower court. This implies that the stigma attached to the conviction and rigour of sentence are completely obliterated. But it does not mean that the effect of conviction and sentence of the lower court is obliterated until the order of conviction and sentence are set aside by the Appellate Court. The conviction and sentence operate pending decision on the appeal for the purpose of the disqualifications provided for under Sub-section (1) of Section 139 of the Act in the case of the O.P. This will be further clear from the reading of clause (g) of Sub-section (1) of Section 139 of the Act. The above clause does not refer to actual imprisonment of the accused as many times the Trial Court may convict and sentence the accused and also may grant provisional bail instantly to allow the accused to file an appeal and it is quite possible that the provisional bail granted by the Trial Court is confirmed by the Appellate Court. Thus the order of conviction and sentence for a term exceeding six months, with or without actual imprisonment, is adequate for the purpose of attracting provision of disqualification provided for in the above sub-clause and grant of bail, *ipso facto*, has nothing to do with the question of disqualification.

12. The learned counsel of the O.P. has referred to the provisions of Sub-section (4) of Section 8 of the R.P. Act, 1951 dealt with by the Hon'ble Supreme Court (*supra*). As would be seen that the relevance of the above provision of the RP Act cited by the learned counsel would prevail in the absence of a specific provision in the Bihar Panchayat Raj Act, 1993. As has been stated earlier, clause (g) of Sub-section (1) of

Section 139 of the Act makes it very clear that the disqualification would continue until the sentence or order has been subsequently reversed. In the face of such a clear cut provision in the Act itself an analogy of the R.P. Act would be totally misplaced. Moreover, as observed in paras 4 to 7 above, the provisions of Sub-section (1) and Sub-section (2) of Section 139 of the Act should be read together and not in isolation and, therefore, the analogy of disqualification before election or after election under the R.P. Act would not be relevant in the instant case which is regulated by a clear and unambiguous provision of clause (g) of Sub-section (1) of Section 139 of the Act. Therefore, this argument of the learned counsel cannot be accepted.

13. The learned counsel of the O.P. has also argued that a writ petition CWJC No. 10697/2002 challenging the validity of Rule 122 of the Rules has been filed in the Patna High Court and the matter has been listed for consideration by a Division Bench and that the O.P. has also filed an I.A. in the High Court on the same issue and, therefore, decision in this case should be deferred till a final decision is taken by the Hon'ble High Court about the validity of Rule 122. Any citizen of this country is free to challenge any piece of law before the appropriate court. But till the law in question is in force its provision would apply. As on date Rule 122 is a valid piece of the Rules and, therefore, the Commission would be perfectly justified to decide the instant case under the above noted rule. Hence the submission of the learned counsel cannot be sustained.

14. The learned counsel of the O.P. has also argued that the remedy in such a case lies in filing an election petition under Section 140 of the Act. It is relevant to mention here that the Commission is not hearing any election petition as it is not competent to do so. An election can be declared as void by the prescribed authority, in this case the concerned Munsif Magistrate, on various grounds as enumerated under Section 144 of the Act. Besides the question of disqualification under the Act, there are other grounds including corrupt practices, for which the Munsif Magistrate can declare the election itself

as void. The question for decision before the Commission is whether the said O.P. suffers from the disqualification under Sub-section (1) (g) of Section 139 of the Act. This power has been delegated to the Commission under Rule 122 of the Bihar Panchayat Election Rules, 1995 (Rules) as notified by the Government *vide* No. 2Pa/VI3-444/2001/657/G.P. dated 28th February, 2002 under the provisions of Sub-section (2) of Section 139 of the Act. The Commission is exercising the power vested in it under Rule 122 of the Rules read with Sub-section (2) of Section 139 of the Act. Thus the issue for decision before the Commission is different from the issue to be decided in an election petition by the competent court of law. The Commission is, therefore, perfectly justified in deciding the question of disqualification, if any, of any person under rule 122 read with Sub-section (2) of Section 139 of the Act. Hence the submission of O.P. cannot be sustained.

15. The learned counsel of the O.P. has also argued that his client was implicated in a false case out of personal rivalry.The Commission is neither a Trial Court nor an Appellate Court to comment on the merit of the order passed by the Sessions Court giving rise to the instant disqualification against the O.P. For the Commission it is enough that the order of conviction and sentence for a term exceeding six months has been passed by a Criminal Court which has attracted the disqualification under clause (g) of Sub-section (1) of Section 139 of the Act and, therefore, the instant case comes within the purview of Rule 122 of the Rules. Hence the submission of the learned counsel cannot be accepted.

16. From what has been stated hereinbefore it would be clear that the provisions of Sub-section (1) and Sub-section (2) of Section 139 of the Act should be read together and not in isolation and, therefore, the O.P. Sri Satya Narayan Dubey comes within purview of clause (g) of Sub-section (1) of Section 139 of the Act and, hence, the question of his disqualification under Rule 122 of the Rules read with Sub-section (2) of Section 139 of the Act should be decided accordingly. It is also proved beyond doubt that the order of conviction and sentence for a term exceeding six months passed by the

Sessions Judge, Buxar referred to earlier has not been reversed by any competent court of law and, therefore, the O.P. Sri Satya Narayan Dubey suffers from the disqualification within the meaning of clause (g) of Sub-section (1) of Section 139 of the Act.

17. Under the circumstances stated above, the State Election Commission, in exercise of its power under Rule 122 of the Rules read with Sub-section (2) of Section 139 of the Act, hereby orders that the O.P. Sri Satya Narayan Dubey shall be disqualified for holding the post of Member of Simari Panchayat Samiti within the meaning of clause (g) of Sub-Section (1) of Section 139 of the Act. In other words, the said Sri Satya Narayan Dubey shall cease to hold the post of Member of the above Panchayat Samiti and to function as such Member. The post of Member of Simari Panchayat Samiti to which the O.P. was elected shall be deemed to be vacant till the said post is filled in accordance with the provisions of the Act.

This order shall take effect from the date of its receipt by the Block Development Officer, Simari.

Index